NEITHER TOLERATION NOR FAVOUR

Neither Toleration nor Favour

THE AUSTRALIAN CHAPTER
OF JEWISH EMANCIPATION

ISRAEL GETZLER

Professor of History
La Trobe University, Melbourne

MELBOURNE UNIVERSITY PRESS

First published 1970
Printed in Australia by
Halstead Press, Kingsgrove, N.S.W. 2208 for
Melbourne University Press, Carlton, Victoria 3053
Great Britain and Europe: ISBS Inc., London
USA and Canada: ISBS Inc., Zion, Illinois 60099
Registered in Australia for transmission by post as a book
Designed by Norman Quaintance

ISBN 0 522 83961 4
Dewey Decimal Classification Number 301.45296094

To the memory
of my Father and Teacher

Acknowledgments

I hope that the many scholars, archivists, librarians and keepers of synagogue records who helped to make this book possible will forgive me if I thank them collectively, naming only those to whom I am especially indebted. Above all I am grateful to my father and teacher, Hayim Mordekhai Getzler who inspired this study and prepared me for it. I sadly regret that he did not live to see the book published, and I have dedicated it to his cherished memory.

I also wish to pay tribute to the sadly missed J. L. O'Brien of the University of Melbourne who taught, trained and encouraged me and supervised the M.A. thesis upon which this study is based.

If J. S. Gregory's seminal masterpiece, 'Church and state in Victoria, 1851-1872', still unpublished, was the model that guided me, Alan McBriar and Hugh Stretton helped me along in so many ways and also made this text more readable and intelligible. I am deeply grateful to them.

I am indebted to Professors Salo W. Baron, Frank Crowley, B. J. Dalton, Shmuel Ettinger, Jonathan Frankel, Ken Inglis, Yakov Katz, Allan Martin, Ezra Mendelson, Douglas Pike, Russel Ward and Dr G. F. J. Bergman who gave generously of their time to comment on sections of the manuscript.

Mrs Bea Wilcock, Mrs Renate Errey and Miss Sue Summerhayes typed successive versions of the text. I wish to thank them for their kindness and patient care.

My final thanks are due to my excellent editor Mrs Camilla Raab for the wise patience and great expertise with which she has treated me and my manuscripts.

Contents

Preface

Jews were not persecuted in the early Australian colonies. They had civil and political rights and religious freedom, but they did not have full religious equality and they worked continuously until they got it. This monograph records those efforts. State aid for their religion may seem a minor matter compared with the equalities Jews elsewhere were still lacking and seeking. But state aid came to have a wider, symbolic importance, as a sign that equality was complete, and the struggle for it came to signify, for many liberal Australians, their part in a wider struggle for Jewish rights elsewhere. This is not a history of Australian Jews in the colonial period; it tells only of their struggle for the removal of one inequity from the public and official arrangements of New South Wales, Van Diemen's Land and Victoria in the 1840s and 1850s; it includes South Australia where that inequity was nipped in the bud, but ignores Queensland and Western Australia where it never existed.

The 'sole grievance' of Jews in colonial Australia appears trifling only when looked at as a mere Australian phenomenon. It gains in significance and weight when viewed against the wider background of mid-nineteenth-century Jewish history: the vicissitudes of Jewish emancipation in Europe, especially in the post-1848 years of counter-revolution, the protracted fight of Jews in England for equal political rights and the coming to self-consciousness of the Jewish people in the aftermath of the 'Damascus blood libel' of 1840. Seen in this perspective, the struggle of Jews in the Australian colonies for religious equality may be regarded as the Antipodean extension of a world-wide movement towards Jewish emancipation and as an integral part of nineteenth-century liberalism.

1

Moreover, since the struggle for the extension of state aid to Jewish religion was waged against the concept of the Christian state, it constituted one catalytic element in the movement towards the separation of church and state and became a minor divisive issue in the conflict between aggressive colonial liberalism and defensive conservatism.

Looked at from both the world-wide and the 'narrow', specifically Australian, points of view, it is the main thesis of this book that the struggle of Jews in Australia for an equitable share in state aid to religion was the Australian version or chapter of Jewish emancipation.

1

Jews in the Age of Liberalism and Emancipation

Ever since the American and French revolutions had proclaimed the doctrine of the natural rights of man and of his equality, Jews in the advanced countries of the west were at some time or other waging a struggle for equal civil, political and religious rights. For in the new commercial and industrial, bourgeois and liberal order which increasingly engulfed the societies of western and central Europe, Jews did remarkably well for themselves: their distinctly urban and commercial mode of life, intellectual traditions and international connections proved to be great assets in the dynamic and competitive conditions of rising capitalism and the modern liberal-bourgeois society and state. Small wonder that Jewish brokers and investment bankers, merchants and industrialists, professionals and men of letters made their fortunes and marks in financial and intellectual capitals such as London, Paris, Amsterdam, Frankfurt, Hamburg and Vienna, and soon graduated into the front ranks of the prosperous and rising middle classes.

Emboldened by their economic success and improved social position and encouraged by the prevalence of liberal-democratic ideas—the 'spirit of the age'—Jews set out to do away with the obvious and painful discrepancy which existed between their new economic and social position and their inferior legal and political status, a legacy from that society of estates which the modern national state was committed to liquidate. They appealed to and prodded the new state to emancipate them, i.e. to legislate for the complete removal of all remaining legal restrictions and political disabilities and for the recognition of their full rights as citizens.

Before 1830, revolutionary or Napoleonic states had sometimes dispensed Jewish emancipation as a boon from *above* (as in revolutionary America and France or in the Rhineland, the Netherlands

3

and Italy under Napoleonic government). Elsewhere, privileged groups of Jewish merchants and bankers had sometimes interceded for the separate or *partial* removal of Jewish disabilities—as with the Jews of Bordeaux in 1790 or those of Berlin in 1799 and 1810.[1] But it was from the 1830s onwards that emancipation became the active and central concern of Jewish life in the west. In England the 'ardent desire of the Jewish nation' for emancipation[2] found its expression in the parliamentary struggle which began in earnest in April 1830 with Robert Grant's unsuccessful Jewish Relief Bill. In Germany the passionate Gabriel Riesser, a leading German-Jewish liberal, scorned the undignified Jewish tactics of lobbying for partial concessions and launched in 1830 an organized open campaign for equal citizen rights.[3] In France the July revolution of 1830 brought Jews positive religious equality when 'ministers of the Israelite cult' were put on the payroll of the state on a par with Christian clergymen.[4] This precedent could only sharpen the determination of Jews elsewhere to rid themselves of humiliating disabilities and to achieve equality at all levels.

A little emancipation increased the need for more. Once educated and liberated from the Ghetto, many Jews in the west lost something of the community and security which membership in an autonomous Jewish corporate body or 'nation' had given them. So they craved for the full alternative, acceptance into European society. Yet the endless and often unexpected difficulties, humiliations and reverses which they encountered in the struggle for equality could only sting and sharpen their sense of insecurity and bewilderment and make them obsessively sensitive to signs of approval and recognition from the Gentile world about them. Attracted by and yet not given a clearly defined status in western society, Jews in the era of Jewish emancipation seem to have responded in somewhat contradictory ways to the ambiguous situation in which they found themselves. On the one hand they appear to have been moved by a compelling urge towards self-denial and fullest assimilation: to become true Frenchmen, Germans, Italians or Englishmen of the 'Mosaic persuasion' was the professed ideal of those who recoiled from going the whole way of the *Taufjude*, of accepting conversion, the 'entrée ticket into civil society' as Heinrich Heine, Germany's satirical poet, called it. On the other hand, the common experience of struggling together for Jewish rights, of defending already conquered yet insecure positions, and of suffering from time to time some serious setbacks on the road towards equality, heightened the feeling of kinship and solidarity with Jews all over the world. This was especially the case in the years which followed upon the 'Damascus affair' of 1840 when, with the connivance of Adolphe Thiers, the 'son of the revolution', and the government of enlightened France, the leading Jews of Damascus were falsely accused and tortured for the murder of the Capuchin Father Thomas de Cammangiano and the alleged use of his blood—'to the last drop'—for Passover cakes. There were more years of reaction after the 1848 revolutions had failed, when many of the achievements of Jewish emancipation in Austria, Italy and a number of German states were either revoked or severely limited.

Such major reverses had shattering effects on Jews at large, including those who had become estranged. They appear in Heinrich Heine's indignant 'Damascus Letters'.[5] The young Ferdinand Lassalle's 'most cherished dream of leading the Jews arms in hand and making them independent' turned into impotent rage.[6] Above all they may be seen in the bitter agony of the 'Communist Rabbi' Moses Hess's *Rome and Jerusalem*:

> Then [in 1840] it dawned upon me for the first time, in the midst of my socialistic activities that I belonged to my unfortunate, slandered, despised, and dispersed people. And already then, though I wanted to express my Jewish patriotic sentiment in one cry of anguish; it was unfortunately immediately stifled in my heart by a greater pain which the suffering of the European proletariat evoked in me.[7]

In the 1840s and 1850s there were signs which pointed to the birth of a new Jewish self-consciousness that began to compete or co-exist with a craving for assimilation into the western nations. At the sentimental level a host of proto-Zionist schemes of Jewish colonization in Palestine aimed at the 'restoration of the Jews'.[8] Quaint proto-Zionist sentiment gave way to serious and concerted political and charitable action by privileged western Jewish communities headed by the Board of Deputies of British Jews and the Alliance Israélite Universelle of France on behalf of persecuted and poverty-stricken Jews in the near east and eastern Europe. Champions of the Jews of Damascus, Moses Montefiore and the Board of Deputies of British Jews, were recognized as 'Defenders of the Jewish Nation',[9] and intervened on behalf of Jews in the Turkish empire, Russia, Morocco, Greece, Persia and Romania. The new spirit of self-conscious international Jewish solidarity informed the Anglo-Jewish newspapers, the *Voice of Jacob* and the

Jewish Chronicle. Founded in 1841 and pledged to 'the defence of Jewish institutions', the Anglo-Jewish press began as a direct and bitter response to the traumatic experience of the Damascus affair when, in the words of the first issue of the *Voice of Jacob*, 'a most formidable attack upon them through the press was spread far and wide, and remained for a long period unanswered'.[10]

Thus when the Jewish emancipation movement in the 1840s and 1850s entered its final phase in western Europe, it received an additional impetus from an awakened Jewish self-consciousness which by the 1860s matured into the first signs of modern Jewish nationalism. Small wonder then that to the Jewish communities in the west, 'the great question of questions'[11] was Jewish emancipation, and the struggle for equality became a central formative experience.

In the larger framework of modern European history, the movement towards Jewish emancipation has been a constant though minor theme, a distinct Jewish contribution to the development of a modern inclusive and democratic-egalitarian society. Forming a classical minority-group, universal, ill defined, often alien in character or mere appearance, more than often unpopular if not hated, Jews when claiming and clamouring for equal rights did so in the name of a general principle, that of the rights of any minority to full equality. As an editorial of the *Jewish Chronicle* in 1852 declared:

> If our body is so small in number, the principle for which we contend is a mighty one! It is the right of every one to worship God in accordance with his honest conscientious convictions, without being subjected to penalties or degrading disabilities . . . This principle is so righteous that thousands of our Christian fellow-citizens would lend us their sympathy and their assistance, did we but prove our desire to enlist them in our cause.[12]

There were many groups in nineteenth-century European society, liberals and democrats, radicals and socialists, Protestant dissenters and minority-Catholics, secularists and anti-clericals, who for one reason or another supported the Jews' struggle for emancipation. Some even, in spite of themselves, became champions of Jewish emancipation. Thus Karl Marx consented in 1843 to draft an emancipation Petition for the Jews of Cologne to the *Landtag* regardless of his own 'distaste for the Jewish faith'. His purpose was, so he wrote to his friend Arnold Ruge, to 'poke as many holes as possible into the Christian state and smuggle into it as much reason as possible.'[13] For the sake of the *general principle* of equality poor Richard Wagner suppressed his antisemitic feelings and fought for *Jewish* equality in the 1848 revolution. In 1850 he ruefully confessed:

> When we fought for the emancipation of the Jews we virtually were more the champions of an abstract principle than of a concrete case . . . our zeal for Jewish equal rights was far more stimulated by a general idea than by real sympathy; for though we strove for Jewish emancipation from the platform and through the press, whenever we came into real active contact with Jews we always felt somewhat repelled.[14]

The most consistent supporters of Jewish emancipation, however, were liberals of many complexions who set out to do away with outdated privileges and disabilities based on estate, religion and tradition and never tired of proclaiming the principles that all citizens were equal before the law and that the state should treat all religious denominations equally. These principles were translated into short-lived legislative action during the liberal spring of 1848–9 when in Austria and Hungary, Prussia and the German States, Denmark, Italy and Sardinia, Jews received equal rights.[15]

In England in the age of the Parliamentary Reform Bills the emancipation of dissenters in 1828, of Catholics in 1829 and of Jews in 1845 and 1858[16] was largely due to the efforts of Whigs, liberals, and philosophical radicals and some evangelicals from the London Society; and generally to the spread of liberal ideology. It was consistently opposed by conservatives of many shades who based their advocacy of a church establishment and of a Christian state on a belief in the duty of the state to promote the *truth* to the exclusion of dissenting 'error', Catholic 'delusion' and Jewish 'blasphemy'.

The first sustained agitation for the removal of Jewish civil and political disabilities began in England in 1830 soon after the repeal of the Test and Corporation Acts in 1828 and Catholic emancipation in 1829; until then political disabilities had been shared by Jews, Protestant dissenters and Roman Catholics.[17] Now Jews were worse off than before. For the new declaration for public office, which since 1828 and the repeal of the Test and Corporation Acts replaced the sacramental test, contained the words 'on the true faith of a Christian'. This phrase had been deliberately reinserted by a rearguard amendment moved by the Bishop of Llandaff in the House of Lords to debar Jews from occupying the municipal and Crown offices now thrown open to dissenters and Catholics.[18]

B

The struggle for the removal of Jewish civil and political disabilities in England lasted over thirty years, and because of the pre-eminent position of British Jewry, commanded the attention of Jews all over the world[19] and especially that of Jews in the Australian colonies.

The arguments for and against Jewish emancipation put forward by liberals and conservatives during the many debates in the House of Commons and the House of Lords are of special interest in so far as they resemble, or are echoed in, the views expressed in the Australian colonial legislatures regarding the extension of state aid to the Jewish religion. Moreover, in their capacity as secretaries of state for the colonies, some of the most notable participants in the debate on the Jewish question in England, e.g. Lord Stanley, W. E. Gladstone, Earl Grey and Lord John Russell, had some considerable influence on the fate of Jewish claims to religious equality in the Australian colonies.

Whether struggling for political rights in England or religious rights in Australia, Jews were confronted by a widely accepted notion of the religious nature and duties of a Christian state. During the debate on the Jews' Declaration Bill in March 1841 Gladstone expressed the views of those who opposed the admission of Jews to Parliament less from anti-Jewish prejudice than from the standpoint of the Christian state. Like Edmund Burke, S. T. Coleridge and Thomas Arnold before him, Gladstone argued that the aim and end of government was not merely the satisfaction of material needs but the 'promotion of true religion and the glory of God'.[20] From this premiss he concluded that

> the profession of the Jews . . . who as conscientious men rejected Christianity as a fable and imposture . . . was of itself in the nature of a disqualification for legislative office in a country where Christianity was interwoven with the institutions of the State.[21]

Eighteen years later the House of Lords, still obstructing as usual one of the many 'Jew Bills' passed by the House of Commons, declared:

> the Lords consider that the denial and the rejection of that Saviour in whose name each House of Parliament daily offers up its collective prayers for the divine blessing on its councils, constitutes a moral unfitness to take part in the legislation of a professedly Christian community.[22]

We shall find similar views on the nature and duties of a Christian state put forward by Sir John Franklin and Sir John

Eardley-Wilmot as Lieutenant-Governors of Van Diemen's Land,
by Richard Cowper, James Martin and James Macarthur in the
Legislative Council of New South Wales and by a solid phalanx of
champions of a Christian state in the Legislative Council of
Victoria.

On the other hand, liberals, philosophical radicals and Irish
rebels like Thomas Babington Macaulay, Joseph Hume, George
Grote, James Mackintosh, Thomas Spring-Rice, Daniel O'Connell,
Benjamin Hawes and Lord John Russell[23] disputed the Christian
and even the religious nature of the state and urged in the name of
religious liberty and equality that Jews be given equal civil and
political rights.

The most distinguished frontal attack on the 'Christian state'
argument against Jewish emancipation came in Macaulay's maiden
speech in 1830:

> Government exists for the purpose of keeping the peace, for the
> purpose of compelling us to settle our disputes by arbitration instead
> of settling them by blows, for the purpose of compelling us to supply
> our wants by industry instead of supplying them by rapine. This is
> the only operation for which the machinery of government is peculi-
> arly adapted, the only operation which wise governments ever
> propose to themselves as their chief object.[24]

Having defined the 'end of government' as exclusively secular and
postulating in words unmistakably Benthamite that 'every man
has a right to all that may conduce to his pleasure', including the
right to hold power, Macaulay denounced 'the infliction of any
penalties on account of religious opinions' as nothing less than
persecution and urged 'on every principle of moral obligation . . .
that the Jew has a right to political power'.[25] In the same vein, and
almost in the same words, a resolution of the House of Commons
twenty-eight years later denounced Jewish disabilities as 'contrary
to the general maxims of freedom of conscience' and declared that

> the infliction of disabilities upon any class of Her Majesty's subjects,
> solely on the ground of their conscientious adherence to their faith,
> savours of persecution, and is totally inconsistent with those principles
> of religious liberty, which, in the case of more powerful communities
> have been applied by Parliament with such happy effects.[26]

While supporters of Jewish emancipation generally saw it as a
question of 'religious liberty', not all were prepared to follow
Macaulay, Joseph Hume or Daniel O'Connell who urged the
secular view of the state which must not 'inquire into the religious

opinions of any individual' because they were irrelevant to politics.[27] Some champions of Jewish equality, like the evangelical
Robert Grant, the Unitarian W. J. Fox and the 'Hebrew' Christian
Benjamin Disraeli, met on their own ground those who rested
their opposition to Jewish emancipation on the assumed duties of
the Christian state.[28] They harped on the Jewish ancestry of
Christianity. As Robert Grant urged when moving for the removal
of Jewish disabilities in 1830:

> The very foundations of our religion were in the religious books of the
> Jews—in those books its principles were to be discovered, and the
> sincere professor of Christianity was deeply implicated in the past
> history and the future estimation of the Jewish people . . . both
> religions had their origin from the same source, and owed their
> existence to the same authority . . . they were not distinct and dis-
> similar religions, but were identical—they were one and the same—
> Judaism was infant Christianity and Christianity was adult Judaism.[29]

Similarly, the Bishop of Chichester in the House of Lords defined
Jews as 'elder brothers of Christians' and urged the removal of
their disabilities,[30] while Disraeli told the House of Commons that
'because this is a Christian assembly and this is a Christian country,
that the Jews ought to find a reception among you'.[31]

Both the secular arguments of Macaulay *and* the religious argu-
ments of Grant seem to have formed the main stock-in-trade of
Australian liberals and radicals who championed Jewish claims to
a share in state aid to religion. William Charles Wentworth and
Robert Lowe in New South Wales during the 1840s and William
Westgarth, Henry Miller and John Pascoe Fawkner in Victoria
during the 1850s spoke the language and expressed the spirit of
English liberalism.

If in England from the 1830s onwards Jews, as before them
dissenters and Catholics, had to struggle for equal civil and political
rights—especially the right to enter Parliament—this was far less
the case in the British colonies. There both dissenters and Jews
faced far fewer restrictions than in the home country. For British
colonial policy, in contrast to that of the Spanish and French, did
not aim at religious uniformity.[32] By offering religious tolerance
and rights of citizenship to all prospective settlers except Catholics,
Britain encouraged the immigration of dissenters, European
Protestants and Jews into its colonies.

The Plantation Act of 19 March 1740 in its preamble embodied
the policy of inducing 'many foreigners and strangers . . . to come

and settle in some of His Majesty's Colonies in America' and offered them citizenship after a term of seven years' residence. It exempted Quakers and Jews from taking the oaths of naturalization in the prescribed form.[33]

In New South Wales Governor Sir Richard Bourke took it for granted that to a 'New Country' like New South Wales, 'persons of all religious persuasions are invited to resort' and that therefore 'a dominant and endowed Church' was out of place.[34]

In Jamaica in 1826 and in Lower Canada in 1831 Jews were given all political rights[35] at a time when in the 'mother country', according to Robert Grant's statement of 1830:

> Jews could not hold any office civil or military, could not be school-masters or ushers, could not be serjeants at law, barristers, solicitors, pleaders, conveyancers, attorneys or clerks, could not be members of Parliament, nor could they vote for return of Members, if anybody chose to enforce the Oath; they were excluded from all corporate offices.[36]

In the Australian colonies Jews appear from the beginning to have enjoyed full civil and political rights: they acquired British nationality, voted at elections, held commissions in the local militia,[37] were elected to municipal offices and were appointed justices of the peace. A Jew, Lionel Samson, was nominated to the Western Australian Legislative Council in 1849, prominent Jews like Saul (later Sir Saul) Samuel and Jacob Levi Montefiore became members of the legislatures of New South Wales in 1854 and 1856 and Morris Marks was elected to the Legislative Council of South Australia in 1857. Thus Jews were found in the legislatures of Australia *before* the Jewish Relief Act of 1858 enabled English Jews to enter the House of Commons.

Yet though Jewish equality was taken for granted and in practice Jews enjoyed equal political rights, there was no legal enactment to sanction their equality. In New South Wales the Chief Justice Alfred Stephen seems to have taken the Plantation Act of 1740 as the authority for allowing Jews who were required to deliver the oath of abjuration for purposes of naturalization or as an oath of office to omit the objectionable part of the oath.[38] Rumours, spread at the time when Saul Samuel stood for election in 1854 that being a Jew he could not enter the legislature,[39] may be taken as some indication that the legal status of Jews had not yet been clearly defined.

Whereas in a legal and political sense Jews in the Australian colonies were equal with their Christian fellow-settlers, this was not the case so far as their religious status was concerned, except in South Australia. They were not of course alone in this, for as long as the Church of England, by virtue of the Church and School Corporation of 1826, was the privileged if not the established church in New South Wales, all non-Anglican denominations shared religious inequality.

Sir Richard Bourke's Church Act of 1836[40] changed all this when it put the Christian denominations on an equal footing with regard to state aid to religion and thus disestablished the Church of England. The preamble of the Act, however, committed it to 'the advancement of the Christian religion' and had the practical effect of excluding Jews from state aid. Nevertheless, whenever Jewish groups applied to the governor of the day for grants of land for burial places, synagogues or Jewish schools, their requests were normally complied with, except in Van Diemen's Land where the Lieutenant-Governor, Sir John Franklin, refused. Moreover, the Constitution Act of 1842,[41] under Schedule C of which state aid was disbursed, referred to 'Public Worship' and thus gave rise to some doubt as to the validity of the Christian limitation implied by Bourke's Church Act. In practice, however, for many years to come, Jews in New South Wales, Van Diemen's Land and Victoria,[42] despite their numerous protests, were excluded from that state aid which all Christian denominations could claim and would receive.

As we shall have ample occasion to see, Jews in the Australian colonies regarded their exclusion from state aid as an act of outright discrimination. In the era of Jewish emancipation, especially during the self-conscious 1840s and 1850s, this is not surprising. Though their actual grievance may not have amounted to very much in practical terms, it was the principle of Jewish religious equality which they sought to establish when clamouring for a share in state aid. Moreover, as there was no legal enactment which officially confirmed the equality of Jews in the Australian colonies at a time when this equality was still in jeopardy abroad, Jews came to regard the admission of their religion to the rank of a state-supported religion as tantamount to such official confirmation.

Thus while the form of the struggle involved a specific religious grievance or disability, it was in fact the means by which the principle of Jewish equality in all spheres and at all levels was to be established. All their numerous petitions and addresses to the various legislatures, governors, secretaries of state and to the Queen seem motivated by one invariable and openly professed aim: to have the principle recognized, in the words of a Jewish resolution on general education in New South Wales of 1844, that 'as British subjects the Israelites of this colony are entitled to the same rights of civil, political and religious liberty which their fellow subjects of different religious opinions enjoy'.[43] In 1846 Sydney Jews solicited support from the London Board of Deputies of British Jews in a letter which was still more explicit. It read:

> any aid we may procure from the Government will be the means of advancing our condition and importance in colonial society; for if the principle be once recognized that the Jewish religion shall receive the same State support that the Christians are entitled to it will give us a political standing in religious matters, and as there are no political distinctions with regard to our civil rights, we should then be placed upon perfect equality with the rest of our fellow citizens.[44]

If their Gentile champions and allies in the Australian colonies spoke the language of English liberalism, Australian Jews, the 'distant remnant of the scattered flock',[45] as they referred to themselves, thought and spoke in terms of the European Jewish emancipation movement. Whether they had settled in New South Wales, Van Diemen's Land, South Australia or Victoria, their group objective was invariably the same—religious equality, even though the form or rather the 'temperature' of their struggle might vary according to local conditions. The colonial Jewish communities seem to have waged the struggle spontaneously and independently of each other, for there is hardly any sign that it was centrally directed or that there was any inter-colonial consultation.

In the chapters which follow we shall see how Jews in the various Australian colonies did 'advance their condition and importance in colonial society' and in the later 1850s achieve the ultimate goal of many a minority group—perfect equality, at least before the law and in the eyes of the state.

The Founding Fathers in New South Wales
1788-1844

The reader of the London police-magistrate Patrick Colquhoun's account of the criminal classes of London during the last decades of the eighteenth century[1] will not be at all surprised to find a small contingent of Jewish convicts in the First and Second Fleets that set sail for Botany Bay in 1787 and 1790 and thereafter a steady trickle of Jewish convicts flowing into the colony of New South Wales until the cessation of transportation in 1840.

While the total number of Jewish convicts who were shipped to and arrived in New South Wales is difficult to assess, it has been estimated that some eight hundred to one thousand arrived in all Australian colonies.[2] For the purpose of this study, however, it suffices to know that in 1828 there were about one hundred Jewish convicts and ex-convicts and some eight free Jewish settlers in New South Wales[3] and that of the 477 Jews that were in the colony in 1836 no less than 300 to 330 were serving convicts or emancipated ex-convicts.[4]

Those Jewish convicts who did land in New South Wales before 1836 and on whom information was available to me seem to have come chiefly from London.[5] Many very poor Jews fled to London from the villages of Poland, Bohemia and Moravia and the Ghettos of Germany and Italy during the latter part of the eighteenth century, trying to escape persecution and oppressive legislation.[6] To these refugees England, with its relative freedom for Jews and its wealthy Jewish upper class of financiers and brokers known for their charity, must have appeared a very haven and 'Eldorado'.[7] However the Jewish immigrants from the continent soon found their hopes for a more decent life shattered, for there were too many of them for the obviously limited charity of some two hundred wealthy Jewish families.[8] The number of Jews in England during the last three decades of the eighteenth century is believed to have jumped from some 6,000–8,000 to 20,000–25,000. Of these, 15,000–20,000 are estimated to have lived in London.[9] Moreover, as a bequest from their Ghetto past in the more backward areas of Europe, they had arrived without technical skills but encumbered by rigid dietary laws and a strict Sabbath observance which prevented their children from acquiring useful trades as apprentices and servants with Christian masters and thus, as Colquhoun hoped, establishing themselves in 'honest employment' and 'mixing with the general mass of the population'.[10] The sons of the Jewish immigrants took to the streets and highways of London and of some provincial towns as orange boys, errand boys, pedlars and buyers of metal and of old clothes, and soon fused—though as a somewhat autonomous section—with the most miserable and debased part of the English 'lower orders', the *Lumpenproletariat*. Forced to 'exist chiefly by their wits', as Colquhoun observed, they soon graduated into crime. Thieving, pickpocketing, receiving and the circulation of false silver coins—the Irish poor specialized in copper coins—appear to have been the crimes to which the Jewish poor of London chiefly resorted.[11] Of those Jewish convicts on whom full data were available the overwhelming majority appear to have been mere 'sneaksmen' and had been tried for theft (in particular pickpocketing of watches), were English born, i.e. were second- if not third-generation migrants, and were of 'working-class' origin; a majority were young people aged between sixteen and twenty-three. There were hardly any females among them and surprisingly few receivers,[12] though receivers or 'fences' figured large in London Jewish crime.[13] It was apparently difficult to prosecute these 'persons of a more steady and prudent turn', as E. G. Wakefield described them,[14] and to prove that they had bought goods knowing that they were stolen.

Except for some halfhearted and shortlived attempts to establish a Jewish burial society,[15] the Jewish emancipists, ticket-of-leave men and 'government men' or convicts serving in gangs, who formed the bulk of the Jewish population in New South Wales until 1828, do not seem to have evinced any great desire to organize themselves into a Jewish congregation. Most of them were probably young, English-born London paupers convicted for petty theft; as such they would have had scarcely any connection with the congregational life of English Jewry, unless as recipients of charity. For in England, as elsewhere in western Europe, Jewish congregational bodies were dominated exclusively by the upper and middle classes. Membership in the Anglo-Jewish congregations was restricted to the well-to-do *Ba'ale Batim* or privileged members and to those who could afford the rental of a seat and thus become *Toshavim*, or seat-holding 'sojourners'. The poor were regarded as 'strangers' (*Orahim*), and did not belong to the congregation.[16]

In Sydney before 1828 there was no free congregation to belong to. There is passing reference to a group of free Jews having arrived in New South Wales in 1790 from London and the Cape of Good Hope who 'would have settled if they had thought it worth while', but they seem to have left as soon as they came.[17] As for Australia's first free Jewish settler, the colourful and enterprising Barnett Levey who arrived in 1821 to join his brother, the well-to-do emancipist Solomon Levey, and soon established himself as a merchant and later as the founder and director of Australia's first theatre, his Jewish ties were rather tenuous: he married a Protestant and had his children baptized.[18] The twenty or so free immigrants who arrived in the colony before 1827 were wives and children who came to join their convict husbands;[19] other Jewish convicts returned home to their families when their sentences expired; e.g. Benjamin Jacobs who in 1817 was 'victualled during voyage at the expense of the Crown' on H.M. brig *Kangaroo*.[20] Among the Jewish convicts there was no minister, and there is no evidence or likelihood that the Jewish authorities in England took any interest in the fate of a few Jewish convicts in far-away New South Wales.[21] They had more than enough Jewish poor to worry about at home.

In the colony, without marriageable Jewish females, convicts could only marry Christians. This as well as other reasons would tend to estrange them from their Jewish group and past. Jacob Josephson, a Hebrew teacher who arrived in the colony in 1818 and married a Protestant in 1821,[22] seems to have kept aloof from the Jewish congregation when it was founded, while some ten convicts with such names as Moses Jacobs, Aaron Isaac and Lewis Solomon are listed in the November 1828 Census as Protestants. Nor do we hear of any hostile feelings against Jewish convicts among the general body of convicts making for a strengthening of their group-consciousness. The leading role played by Edward Davis in the 'Jew-boy gang' of bushrangers in the 1830s[23] suggests integrative relations between Jewish and Gentile convicts.

Thus with no free Jewish settlers, no Jewish females, no Jewish ecclesiastic, no help from home and no persecution in the colony, the London-Jewish convicts were, as the *Report of the Sydney Synagogue 1845* put it, 'little versed in the faith of their ancestors'.[24] They did not stress their Jewishness, or try to organize, or otherwise set themselves apart from the pronounced collectivism of the general body of convict population.

Common social origins and common afflictions seem to have been stronger than any religious divisions among the 'founding fathers', whether Gentile or Jew.

The first serious and lasting attempt to found a Jewish congregation followed the arrival in the late 1820s and early 1830s of more than one hundred free Jewish settlers.[25] Among these were some well-to-do merchants and financiers from London with longstanding family interests in colonial trade and speculation. There were the wealthy 'Jew broker' Joseph Barrow Montefiore (he bought the privilege in 1826 for £1,500), his partner David Ribeiro Furtado and his brother-in-law George Mocatta, the young Phillip Joseph Cohen who is reported to have had a commission from the London Rothschilds and his partners Lawrence and Stephen Spyer.[26] These, with other middle-class immigrants and tradesmen, were attracted by the new immigration policies and pastoral opportunities of the late 1820s and 1830s, notably by the alluring prospect—certainly novel to Jews—of setting themselves up as landowners on land granted by the Crown. J. B. Montefiore arrived in February 1829, commended by the Treasury as 'a most respectable gentleman and . . . a most valuable acquisition to the Colony'; he was recommended for a grant of 5,000 acres[27] and immediately received 2,560. Others found the welcome less warm. The shoemaker Michael Hyam who arrived at the end of 1828 had first to overcome the deep prejudice of Governor Darling against a 'perfect Jew' *and* a tradesman, before he could receive a grant and become a 'man of landed estate'.[28]

The Governor wrote to Under-Secretary Twiss:

> For my own part, I could wish that such people as Hyam and his partner would confine themselves to their own proper calling, and defer becoming landed Proprietors until they have done making shoes and selling stockings.[29]

Many of the free Jewish settlers had been active in the Jewish congregational life of London, were connected with its leading Jewish families and had many reasons, religious and social as well as commercial and financial, for maintaining their ties with home.

They transplanted the educated, Anglo-Jewish middle class form of congregational life they knew to the Antipodes and thus became the founding fathers of organized Jewish religion and community life in Australia. They were soon joined by a number of Jewish emancipists who had done well for themselves, such as Abraham Elias, James Simmons, Samuel Lyons, Vaiben Solomon and Abraham Polack, and who must have been greatly attracted by the respectability and status of the newly arrived congregation-builders. This is how the *Report of the Sydney Synagogue 1845* described this process:

> In the years 1827 and 1828 the worldly condition of the Hebrews in this Colony had considerably improved from various causes, the influx of respectable merchants during those years coupled with other circumstances had raised the Hebrews in the estimation of their fellow colonists, and it was then thought advisable meetings for prayer should be held regularly . . .[30]

What precisely those 'various causes' and 'other circumstances' were, we have been left to guess. Yet we cannot help noticing in passing how much store was put on the 'estimation' of their non-Jewish fellow-colonists.

Religious services were held in 1829 at the house of P. J. Cohen and Lawrence Spyer in George Street.[31] On 9 April 1830 the *Australian* reported the celebration of the Jewish Passover in the colony 'when the tribe of Israel shut up their shops and will do but little business for four or five days to come', adding 'the quantity of unleavened bread made and likely to be consumed during the present Paschah exceeds already former seasons.' This report is some indication that Jews as a group were already noted and known as shopkeepers and that for some years past unleavened bread had been baked in the colony for the Jewish Passover.

There seems to have been some early 'schism' when one group led by the well-to-do emancipists Abraham Elias and James Simmons would not join in the services conducted by P. J. Cohen because of 'some difference of opinion then existing amongst the members of the faith'.[32] The visit of Rabbi Aaron Levy, a member of the London Rabbinical Court (*Beth Din*), in 1830–1 marked (in the words of the *Report of the Sydney Synagogue 1845*) 'the establishment of our holy religion in this colony on a firm foundation'.[33] Rabbi Levy supplied a Scroll of the Holy Writ (*Sepher Torah*) and prayerbooks, corrected many religious 'errors and abuses that then existed', arbitrated between the two rival congregational bodies and encouraged more regular and unified Jewish activities. A Hebrew Congregation was officially founded in 1832 with J. B. Montefiore as president, Abraham Elias as treasurer and the emancipist George Moss as honorary secretary.[34] A room for a temporary synagogue was hired and in the absence of a Jewish minister, P. J. Cohen acted as religious leader, preaching, reading the weekly sections from the *Sepher Torah* and performing Jewish marriages in the colony, until the arrival in 1835 of a Reader, the Rev. M. E. Rose, with credentials from the London Chief Rabbi, Solomon Hirschell. A Jewish marriage took place in 1832. Ritual circumcision was performed on the newborn in the colony by Simon Lear, an emancipist dentist. In October 1832 the Governor, Sir Richard Bourke, granted land for a Jewish burial-ground.[35]

All this information indicates that by the middle of the 1830s there was a growing Jewish community in the colony, concentrated largely in Sydney. In the Census of 1833, 345 persons had declared themselves as of the Jewish religion. In 1836 their number had increased to 477, of whom 340 were living in Sydney.[36] Many made a living as dealers, shopkeepers, auctioneers, innkeepers, storekeepers and merchants[37] and thus made up a sizeable part of the small commercial class in the colony. They had succeeded in organizing themselves into a religious body with all the proper attributes of a congregation, were recognized as such by the London Chief Rabbi, possessed sufficient confidence to apply to the Governor for a land grant and were sufficiently conspicuous to be noticed by the colonial press.

But when in 1836 Governor Sir Richard Bourke organized state and church relations in the colony,[38] he ignored the Jewish congregation. While his Church Act extended state aid for the building of churches and chapels and the payment of clergymen's salaries to all denominations on equal terms, its preamble contained the phrase 'for the advancement of the Christian religion' and thus excluded the Jewish religion. In his original plan of 1833 for state aid to religion[39] Bourke realized that by 'granting assistance systematically to more than one Church . . . a claim is given for assistance upon the same principle to every Congregation of Dissenters and of Jews', and he left it open to himself or to a future governor to extend state aid to them should they request and require it.[40]

Yet when at last in 1836 the Church Act came and was promptly hailed by Dr John Dunmore Lang's *Colonist* as the 'Magna Charta of the Religious Liberty of this infant Empire',[41] it did make provision for 'every Congregation of Dissenters' but none for the Jews.

Worse still, its preamble became the legal foundation for advo-cates of a Christian state and opponents of Jewish religious equality. In the light of his original plan this cannot have been the real intention of Sir Richard Bourke, an advanced liberal and Whig who as Acting Governor in the Cape of Good Hope 'emancipated the Hottentots'[42] and was connected by a close and life-long friend-ship with Thomas Spring-Rice, the early champion of Jewish emancipation in the House of Commons.[43]

Bourke's intention—and certainly that of his Attorney-General, the O'Connellite Catholic J. H. Plunkett who drafted the Church Act and regarded it as the most important single achievement of his public career[44]—was the disestablishment of the Church of England and the extension of equal religious rights to all Christian denominations, in particular to the Roman Catholics who needed them most and came to look upon Bourke's Church Act as 'the MAGNA CHARTA OF OUR RELIGIOUS RIGHTS AND STANDING'.[45] This aim was achieved by its inclusively Christian preamble which referred to 'Christian Worship', undefined.[46] William Grant Broughton, the Anglican Bishop of Australia, denounced Bourke's religious scheme mainly because it put the Roman Catholic Church on a par with the Churches of England and Scotland and thus would 'check the progress of the Reformation'.[47] Broughton would, as Bourke knew only too well, 'have brought up in array' any opposition he could possibly mobilize. He rubbed in the point that Bourke's scheme would extend religious equality to dissenters and Jews.[48] In these circumstances, Bourke may have feared to endanger the Act by pressing the general principle of religious equality to radical extremes, or by taking into account specifically the future needs of a small Jewish minority. The Jews still had neither rabbi nor synagogue. There is no evidence that they pressed for inclusion into the provisions of the Church Act or felt discriminated against by the Governor. In their farewell address upon his departure from the colony, they expressed their admiration for him and their appreciation of 'the great and liberal spirit of religious toleration that has adorned your Vice-Royalty . . . in disseminating kind and generous feelings between all creeds and sects of Her Majesty's subjects'.[49] In his reply, Bourke declared that he 'was happy to find that his endeavours to establish the principles of civil and religious liberty in the colony upon a permanent basis is duly appreciated by them'.[50]

The difference in tone is unmistakable. While the Whig Governor spoke of 'principles of civil and religious liberty', the Jewish leaders were still satisfied with the 'spirit of religious toleration' Jews had craved in the pre-emancipation era and with the promise of a grant of land for a synagogue. There is no indication that they even thought of challenging the fateful Christian preamble to the Church Act.

The late 1830s were of great moment in the development of the Jewish community in New South Wales. Its numbers more than doubled; by 1841 there were 841 Jews in the colony (462 in Sydney) and in 1846 1,668 (603 in Sydney).[51] They had economic weight, social status and useful connections. While Jacob Montefiore in London was a director of the Bank of Australasia, his brother Joseph was a director of its Sydney branch, and expected to 'handle a quarter million pounds of British capital' in 1835.[52] He has been described as 'a pioneer in the application of English capital to wool-growing',[53] he was an active speculator in land during the pastoral boom of the 1830s. So was the wealthy merchant and auctioneer Samuel Lyons who in 1834 transacted a good half of all private land sales in the colony.[54] So were other leading Jews who bought allotments in Melbourne's earliest land sales.[55] Business partnerships between Jewish and Gentile merchants were quite common, such as that of Solomon Levey with Daniel Cooper, Samuel Lyons with Charles William Wentworth, Jacob Levi Montefiore (a nephew of Joseph) with Robert Graham, a 'pious Scot from Edinburgh'.[56] Both Joseph Montefiore and Samuel Lyons were on the committee of the Australian Patriotic Association when it was founded by W. C. Wentworth in 1835, while Samuel Lyons was also on the committee of the non-denominational Sydney College.

Jews in the colony displayed no less zeal when building up their congregational institutions. We sense their enthusiasm and determination when we learn that in 1839 all Sydney Jews gathered and decided to build a synagogue and solemnly resolved that 'this contemplated work of our hands shall neither be slack nor stop'.[57] When early in 1843 part of the synagogue was completed they thought that they were engaged in nothing less than the building of 'the first place of public worship for the Hebrew nation in the Southern Hemisphere'.[58] We find them looking after their poor, their sick and some Jewish convicts in Norfolk Island,[59] and appointing local representatives of the Sydney Synagogue in a number of country towns: Parramatta, Maitland, Goulburn, Windsor, Monaro, Yass, Five Islands, Moreton Bay, Port Macquarie, Berrima and Hinton.[60] By 1846 Sydney Jews had a congregation consisting

of 80 privileged members and 110 seat-holders, a Burial Society, a
Philanthropic Society, a Ladies' Benevolent Institution, a Beriss
Association (catering for ritual circumcision), Moses Rintel's
private Hebrew School which was open daily from 2-5 and was
attended by some forty pupils, a Reading Society and a library
with some 757 books of Jewish and general interest.[61] At the same
time they kept close contact with Jews in England by private correspondence with relations and business friends there, and kept
themselves informed about the affairs of British and world Jewry
by subscribing to London Jewish journals. The *Voice of Jacob* and
the *Jewish Chronicle* were 'very considerably read'.[62]

George Moss, the indefatigable honorary secretary of the congregation, hailed the *Voice of Jacob* as 'impressive proof that,
destined as [Jews] are to spread abroad throughout the habitable
globe—Israel as a nation, is still One, as is the God it adores, as is
the creed it professes.'[63] He became its Sydney correspondent and
soon published a Sydney edition of *The Voice of Jacob or The
Hebrew Miscellany* which he had printed in the printery of the
Australian (he was the *Australian*'s official printer and publisher)
and distributed free of charge.[64] The Sydney *Voice of Jacob* contained copious extracts from the London journal, and colonial
matters of special interest to the 'scattered sheep of the flock of
Israel' in New South Wales; three numbers appeared before it
closed (at a time of general depression) for lack of financial back-
ing. The journal was not the only casualty of the depression. There
were 'numerous defaults'[65] and a number of Jewish trading houses,
such as the Montefiores, went bankrupt.

While building up their congregational institutions and looking
after their private commercial ventures the Jewish leaders seem to
have been satisfied, at least until 1844, with their position in the
colony. When in 1840 George Moss urged the leaders of the Sydney
Hebrew Congregation to emulate their brethren in Jamaica and
apply for state aid,[66] they did not do so. When in 1842 the Constitution Act (5 & 6 Vic., c.76) allocated an annual sum of £30,000
for 'Public Worship', undefined, the Jewish leaders let the opportunity pass and did not challenge the Christian limitation imposed
by the Church Act.

They were at last shaken out of their complacency in 1844, when
a select committee of the Legislative Council under the chairman-
ship of Robert Lowe, the colony's outstanding liberal spokesman
and thinker, recommended a state-supported non-denominational
but Christian system of education.[67] It should be a National or

Irish system, non-sectarian and 'sufficiently comprehensive to include both Protestants and Catholics'. The Lowe Report distinguished between 'literary and moral education' and 'religious instruction'. The former would be 'ordinary school business', but would include readings from Scripture, i.e. from the Old and New Testaments; the latter would be the business of clergymen or other qualified persons who would instruct on one day set apart for this purpose in each week.[68]

The Jewish community found itself in a dilemma. On the whole, in tune with liberal sentiment in the colony, it favoured a system of general rather than denominational education; the latter might retard the full acceptance and integration of the small Jewish group in a predominantly Christian community. On the other hand, the recommended system of general education had disregarded the very existence of the Jews. The stand they eventually took shows that they regarded the education issue above all as an opportunity to put forward a claim to equal rights. On 17 September 1844 a well-attended public meeting of Sydney Jews protested against their exclusion from the benefits of state-assisted education, whether general or denominational, and adopted resolutions which in combination constituted their first public claim to equal civil, political *and* religious rights.[69]

The first speaker, John J. Cohen, praised the Select Committee of the Legislative Council 'for having brought forward a measure having for its tendency the blessings of the principle of General Education'. He deplored, however, that the Committee had 'lost sight' of the Jewish community and that its report was so framed

> as to preclude the Israelites from an equally free and legitimate participation in the benefits arising therefrom . . . For Jews could not conscientiously send their children to those schools where the general elements of instruction inculcate the tenets and doctrines of the Christian faith.

Nevertheless, he urged Jews to support the proposed system of general education in spite of their misgivings and not to 'hazard an innovation of such vital importance to our civil, political and religious rights'. Likewise, P. J. Cohen, the stalwart founder and leader of the congregation, favoured general education and praised its virtues:

> it would be far better to have a system where all might be taught, where all religious creeds might meet; it would soften that asperity of feeling which now exists between persons of different creeds and

C

would do more to improve the social condition of mankind than anything that has yet been attempted.

Religious education, he thought, should be left to parents and
ministers of religion. Jewish religion in particular was of 'so simple
a nature, the belief in one creator only', that any one could teach
it successfully.

He then moved a resolution which claimed equality for Jews at
all levels and a proportionate share in state-supported education:

> That as British subjects, the Israelites of this colony are entitled to
> the same rights of civil, political and religious liberty which their
> fellow subjects of different religious opinions enjoy, and they there-
> fore consider themselves entitled on grounds of public equity, to a
> proportionate share of advantage from any measure for General
> Education which may be instituted at the public expense, without
> compromising their faith or waiving their paternal rights.

He called upon the assembled Jews to give their unanimous support to the resolutions as the Petition embodying these, which
they were about to present, if granted, 'would place them in that
position of society which they ought long since to have been placed
in'. George Moss alone disagreed with previous speakers:

> For his own part he was bound to state, though it was generally
> disapproved of by his co-religionists, that he himself was far more
> disposed towards the denominational system, than that of a general
> ... as that would give them an opportunity of teaching their children
> agreeably to their own views ...

If he proposed the Petition, none the less he did so rather 'with a
view to establish a right as a British born subject'. He suggested
that Wentworth should be asked to present their Petition to the
Legislative Council, for he could be relied upon to do his best 'to
secure the rights of Englishmen to every man, let his creed be what
it may'. Dissenting about education, Moss still agreed with the rest
of the community that the real issue on this occasion was Jewish
equality.

That being its primary aim, the Petition itself was worded in
such a way as to maintain the right of Jews to a share in state aid
to education, whether a general or a denominational system were
adopted:

> if a General System of Education be adopted by your Honorable
> House and schools in conformity with such a system be established to

which they could conscientiously send their children for the purposes of General Education without interfering with their religious scruples, your memorialists would be perfectly satisfied . . .

This showed their preference for general education,

but should your Honorable House be determined to adopt the system of Denominational Schools as it now exists, your petitioners would humbly pray that they may not be excluded from the benefits arising from such a system and that they may be allowed the same privileges as are now granted to their Christian brethren.[70]

The *Australian*, in spite of its advocacy of denominational education, came out in full support of the Jewish claim and declared that 'no one dreams of denying . . . that "they are entitled to the same rights of civil, political and religious liberty which their fellow subjects of different religious opinions enjoy".' It repeatedly advised Jews to petition for their proper share 'not for Education alone but for purposes of religion also', but criticized their stand in favour of general education.[71]

On 2 October 1844 W. C. Wentworth presented the Jewish Petition to the Legislative Council. He complimented Sydney Jews for lending their support to the general system of education which could not be 'applied to their views' and thus gave 'an example of liberality which was worthy of imitation by their Christian brethren'.[72] From the remarks of Dr Lang, the pugnacious democrat and Presbyterian leader, however, it appears that the Jewish community had been given an assurance by him that in schools to be set up under the general system, Jewish children would be exempted from reading lessons in the New Testament.[73] Nothing came of this plan for general education. Governor Gipps even refused a token grant of £2,000.[74] Since at the time there was no Jewish day-school in the colony, Jews could not ask for state aid to Jewish denominational education. When in September 1845 the establishment of a Jewish school was contemplated, the possibility of applying for state aid was considered and it was thought that they had 'every reason to believe it would be granted'.[75]

Thus it appears that the Jewish community, in tune with liberal opinion in the colony, was in favour of general, non-denominational education. Their main champions and allies were colonial radicals like Wentworth and Lang, advocates of the voluntary principle in religion and of a general, non-denominational system in education. However, the primary object of Jewish intervention in the educational controversy of 1844 was the assertion of equal rights. They seem to have relished the significance of their first stand on a public matter when at long last, as one speaker put it, they 'shook off their apathy and came forward to claim their rights as Englishmen'.[76] This experience was shared by their brethren in far-away London who applauded them and reported this 1844 meeting as 'the most important movement' of Jews in New South Wales.[77] Sydney Jews had come of age as they entered the age of Jewish emancipation.

3

On the Brink of Religious Equality in New South Wales 1845-1846

With its intervention in the education controversy the Sydney Jewish community had come of age, and its leaders felt confident and ready to face the Church Act and force the issue of their exclusion from state aid. The *Report of the Sydney Synagogue 1845* conveys a sense of the importance they attributed to this issue: 'a crisis has now arrived which will if properly followed up lead to important results to the Jewish community, which in after ages will be viewed with gratitude and affection'.[1]

Besides the principle of equality, state aid had some practical attractions. In 1844 when its rather ambitious synagogue building had just been completed, the Jewish congregation was deeply in debt.[2] The colonial government helped to build other churches—why not theirs? Besides some help with the debt, they needed £150 a year to enable them to bring a proper minister from England. Sympathetic newspapers such as the *Examiner* and the *Australian* suggested repeatedly that they petition the Legislative Council for permission 'to partake in the benefits of our Church Act'. The *Examiner* suggested, as a solution to the problem posed by the preamble of the Church Act, that the word 'Christian' be expunged. It struck a hopeful note when it added: 'We know that if the Hebrew religionists will ask for the boon it will be cordially conceded.'[3]

In October 1845 Jews drew up a Petition to the Legislative Council and asked their champion, W. C. Wentworth, to present it.[4] The Petition made the following points:

The Sydney Congregation had been given a grant of land for a synagogue in 1841 but it had proved unsuitable for the purpose. When they applied for permission to sell or to exchange the land, this permission had been refused. They had to buy a piece of land for a synagogue out of their own funds and were now indebted to the tune of £1,000. They had never asked for nor received any financial aid from the government during the fourteen years of their existence. However, as loyal citizens who contributed to the revenue and who paid all taxes and rates in common with their Christian brethren, they felt entitled like them to receive state aid in support of their religious establishments. They referred to Jamaican precedents where the legislature voted several times a sum of £1,000 to assist the Jewish congregation to build and repair their synagogue. They asked for a sum of money to help them liquidate 'the debt now due for building the Synagogue' and for an annual stipend for a Jewish minister. They finally urged that since by Schedule C of the Constitution Act of 1842 £30,000 was allocated annually 'to Public Worship without reference to any particular religion, Jews were entitled to receive a sum of money in proportion to their numbers.'[5]

Wentworth moved on 24 October in the Legislative Council that the Governor be asked to allot from Schedule C £1,000 for the liquidation of the synagogue debt and towards the erection of a house for a Jewish minister; and he moved for an annual sum of £150 as a stipend for a Jewish minister.[6] He urged a unanimous vote in favour of the grant for, whatever might be the ultimate fate of the address, he trusted that the House would show that it possessed sufficient liberality of feeling and a sufficient sense of justice to pass it without dissent. Jews in the colony contributed to the revenue 'at least' as largely as colonists of other denominations, without deriving the same advantages from it. He thought 'there could be no question' that the unfortunate phrase in the 1836 Church Act was overridden by the 1842 Constitution Act which referred only to 'public worship'. Appealing to the spirit of the author against the letter of his Church Act, Wentworth added:

> he was satisfied from what he knew of Sir Richard Bourke's sense of justice that if at the time of the passing of this Act the Jewish people had formed as large a congregation as at present and had claimed to be included in its provisions, their claim would have been acceded to.

The matter was not as unquestionable as Wentworth hoped. Deas Thomson, the Colonial Secretary, quite liberal minded but far more cautious than his father-in-law Sir Richard Bourke, gave the lead to government members and nominees when he insisted that the Church Act was not affected by the Constitution Act and that it was precisely by the provisions of the Church Act that 'the Executive Government, under the advice of its law officers' regulated state aid to religion. He regretted that the Church Act should at all be questioned. It was acceptable to the whole colony 'except perhaps some individuals who might be desirous of seeing the establishment of a Dominant Church'. He was not aware that there were any English precedents for legislative grants to Jewish congregations, except one recent concession to Roman Catholics.[7] He thought it would have been 'less objectionable' if a separate grant from the General Estimates had been asked for.

J. H. Plunkett, the Attorney-General, was certainly more sympathetic. He favoured the 'subject matter' of the motion but insisted that the Church Act was valid,[8] so that even if the motion were passed, 'between the Council and the Church Act, the members of the Jewish persuasion would get nothing'. Plunkett agreed with Wentworth that 'if the petitioners had been sufficiently numerous at the time this Act was passed and had claimed to be included into its provisions, their claim would not have been overlooked'. He would therefore move as an amendment to place the sums of money applied for upon the estimates for 1846 and not to appropriate them out of Schedule C. Dr J. D. Lang as a voluntaryist objected to any increase in state aid as a matter of principle. He would therefore vote for the original motion as 'fair and proper' but would oppose the amendment. Only Charles Cowper, so staunch and exclusive an Anglican that he was known as 'the Member for the Church of England',[9] would oppose both the motion and the amendment since he objected to the 'subject matter'. Even the Church Act could not satisfy him, for he believed that 'it was the duty of the Government to support the truth and the truth only', and to Cowper the 'truth' was vested in the established Church of England. Cowper and Deas Thomson nevertheless went out of their way to make sure their negative votes would not be interpreted as anti-Jewish prejudice. They testified to the 'high character of the Jewish community' and professed to have 'the most kindly feelings towards that class'.

Richard Windeyer, as liberal and aggressively independent as his friend and ally Robert Lowe, took issue with the Colonial Secretary on the question of precedents. He voiced the liberal-colonial point of view which refused to be bound and guided by the precedents and prejudices of England. If there were no precedents they should make one, and comply with 'so just a demand . . . without feeling . . . fettered in any way by the feelings or pre-

judices of the mother country, which had prevented the adoption
of such a course in that quarter'. But precedents were shown to
exist, the government of India even going so far as to assist the
public worship of pagans.

Robert Lowe questioned the validity of the Church Act and
contended that 'every Colonial Act must necessarily be overridden
by . . . the Imperial Act', i.e. the Church Act of 1836 by the Constitution Act of 1842. He even staked a superior claim for Jews to
state assistance:

> The Jews ought to be the first whose claims were attended to: for
> their religion had by far the priority over their Christian brethren.
> Their warriors had ceased to fight, their poets had ceased to sing, and
> their own greatness as a nation had passed away . . .

Jews therefore deserved special consideration.

When the vote was taken, the original motion (Jews to share
in Schedule C) was carried by 8 votes to 5 and J. H. Plunkett's
amendment (Jews to receive a special grant from the general
revenue) was lost by 4 votes to 11. The combined vote in favour
of state aid to Jews was 12 votes to 4.[10]

Two Sydney newspapers warmly welcomed the vote.[11] The
Cumberland Times in a lengthy leader under the title 'The Rights
of the Hebrews' told colonists that they should 'justly feel proud
of the enlightened liberality of our Legislative Council the whole
of whom with one solitary and meanly conspicuous exception'
(Charles Cowper was meant) conceded to the Jews 'an influential
and respectable class of their fellow colonists', their equal rights.
In matters of this nature the practices of the home country afforded
no guidance since they issued 'from self-elected conclaves which
have been sometimes notoriously corrupt, sometimes suspicious
and never wholly unobjectionable.' Mustering a whole array of
Jews who had distinguished themselves in the political life of the
West Indies and in the municipal offices of England, the *Cumberland Times* reiterated the case for full Jewish equality: 'with men
of common sense and common honesty no doubt can exist that the
Hebrews are fully entitled to participate equally with other
religious societies in every benefit and assistance which the State
can afford.'[12]

The *Examiner* also supported the vote. No colonial newspaper
criticized it. In this sin of omission the conservative *Sydney Morning Herald* was taken to task by an angry correspondent who had
'impatiently' but vainly waited for it or some correspondent to pro-

test against this 'gross insult' to the Christian religion. This correspondent who signed himself 'Christianus', modestly adding
'Sed Minimus Inter Christianos',[13] offered the only comprehensive
Christian-state argument voiced on this occasion; he spelt out in
detail what a staunch Christian state man like Charles Cowper
may have preferred to leave unsaid in the Legislative Council.
Moreover, the controversy which 'Christianus' initiated in the
newspapers[14] added significantly to the scant and largely constitutional debate in the Legislative Council.

'Christianus' feared that the vote of the Legislative Council
would 'unchristianize' the government of the colony, therefore 'all
Christians should raise their faithful protest against an innovation
by which a teacher will be paid for traducing the Holy Name of
Jesus and stigmatizing as an imposter the Eternal Son of God.'
The root of the evil was naturally enough Bourke's Church Act:
if the vote was consistent with the spirit of Bourke's Church Act,
as Wentworth and Plunkett had argued, then colonists must have
been 'cherishing in their bosom a viper which concealed a fang
poisoned against the Redeemer himself'. Ridiculing Robert Lowe
for 'eulogizing if not to prefer the Jewish religion on account of its
priority', 'Christianus' drew a sharp distinction between the 'ancient
church of Israel' and the modern Judaism of 'an unbelieving people
who rejected the Messiah at his coming and were by Him rejected'.
Antagonism between Judaism and Christianity being so great, the
government which 'endows both, disowns both and gives direct
sanction to infidelity'. Worse still, having endowed Judaism, he
asked, 'can you stop there' and not endow in due time the Mosque
or the 'sanguinary and immoral superstitions of Juggernaut?'

'Christianus' disposed rather ingeniously of the equitable argument that the state must 'give all who contribute to the public
revenue a share in its appropriations': it was not 'unfair', he urged,
to expect the Jew, a 'citizen of the world' who chose to 'reside
amongst us' seeking 'a fair measure of protection in his dealings',
to contribute his share to the maintenance of 'those [Christian]
influences' by which the 'order, social system . . . and character of
the community' in which he 'chooses to live' is formed.

While denying equality to the Jew on the ground that he lived
in a Christian state, 'Christianus' pleaded for his toleration on the
ground that his presence confirmed Christian truth: the Jew should
not 'in any way' be persecuted or 'needlessly be insulted', nor should
he be discouraged from 'residing among us' for 'his presence is a
most useful auxiliary to the ministers of the Saviour, carrying (as

he does) the proofs of the authenticity of the Old Testament and showing in his own person the fulfilment of prophecy.'[15] All in all, colonial 'Christianus' repeated faithfully some of the stock arguments against Jewish emancipation in England as brought into array by Sir Robert Inglis, the Earl of Winchelsea or Lord Stanley, softening them somewhat in so far as he called the Jew a 'citizen of the world' rather than a 'stranger' who belonged to a 'nation apart' and referred to the Jew's 'dealings' rather than to his 'traffic in money'. In a similar vein, 'A Jew' who wrote to the *Sydney Morning Herald* a letter-in-reply, repeated the stock answers of Jews and liberals 'at home' together with the usual affirmation of 'loyalty' so characteristic of the insecure European Jew in the age of emancipation:

> I deny, gentlemen, in the strongest terms we are a nation apart, any more than members professing the Catholic, Wesleyan, or any other of the numerous sects into which Christianity is divided. A British Jew would defend his country against a foreign Jew if occasion required, with as much alacrity and good feeling as a Christian could possibly do. Why, then, are we to be deprived of our privileges, and branded as men belonging to no country?[16]

'Any more' perhaps weakened his 'strongest terms'. There was some colonial deviation from the well-worn European theme in his sour acceptance of the title 'citizen of the world' and his pointed refusal to 'pass the same compliment' upon 'Christianus' who was 'only a citizen of the Church of Christ'. Perhaps some colonial-egalitarian flavour can be detected in the three letters which 'Humilitas' published in Robert Lowe's *Atlas* and addressed to 'Minimo inter Christianos, Minori inter Logicos':

> The reason which 'Minimus' gives for not persecuting or needlessly insulting the Jew, is very curious. It is not because he is a man and carries about with him the inalienable rights of our common nature to the protection of the laws and institutions to which he contributes, but because 'his presence is a most useful auxiliary'. The Jew is to be preserved as a sort of theological fossil or bijou, in the cabinet of the sacred antiquary . . .[17]

Only one participant in the debate argued for Jewish equality on the ground of the Jew's large stake in colonial reality:

> when it is remembered that the Children of Israel form in this colony an important section of the population, and that they are for the most part industrious, useful and respectable members of the com-

munity, it can scarcely be disputed . . . that their due proportion . . .
for the purpose of public instruction, whether religious or otherwise,
may not be withheld without manifest and glaring injustice.

Colonial 'Christianus' was certainly blind to the novel realities
of colonial society: the unsightly, if not Ahasverian, 'old clothes
Jew' of London in the early decades of the century might have
served as 'a most useful auxiliary' to Christian truth; but was this
true of his prosperous brother in Sydney who seems rather to have
testified to the involuntary blessing of Balaam than to the 'fulfilment of prophecy'?! Judging by the tone of the debate in the
Legislative Council, of the editorials in the newspapers and the
lively controversy in the correspondence columns of the *Sydney
Morning Herald* and of the *Atlas*, 'Christianus' was also largely
out of tune with colonial opinion.

Colonial opinion, however, proved far in advance of the policy
of the colonial government and of the Colonial Office. The *Examiner* had expressed the fear that though the Jews had been
successful in the Legislative Council, they would lose their case
in the Executive Council, where the meaning of Schedule C would
be construed in strict reference to the Church Act.[18] All Crown
officers had voted against the original motion and only two for the
amendment.[19] With the validity of the Church Act in question, it
would have required a very sympathetic Governor to comply with
the Address of the Legislative Council. Sir George Gipps had made
no difficulties when Jews in Sydney and Port Phillip applied for
grants of land for the building of synagogues. There he had the
precedent of Sir Richard Bourke. But on the other hand he had also
Bourke's Church Act which precluded Jews from state aid. Gipps
and his Attorney-General, Plunkett, regarded the Church Act as
valid because it had not been repealed, and acted accordingly
when distributing funds from Schedule C. Their views on this
matter had met with the approval of the Secretary of State for the
Colonies, Lord Stanley.[20] Generally, Gipps appears to have been
less of a liberal in religious and educational matters than his predecessor. He was Bishop Broughton's close friend and seems to
have valued highly 'the opinions and advice of the Lord Bishop'.[21]
During the general education controversy of 1844 he had defeated
all the attempts of the liberal reformers to wrest the control of
education from the churches, even so far as to deny them a token
grant of £2,000 for an experiment. He had also advocated some
measure of preferential treatment for the Church of England,

referring to it as the 'Established Religion of the Empire'.[22] So it was not surprising that he should inform the Legislative Council that he felt he had no authority to comply with their Address. Nor did he show his good will by suggesting some alternative ways in which the Jewish claims could be satisfied, either in his reply to the Legislative Council, or in his despatch to the Secretary of State where he explained his refusal: 'I considered I could not legally appropriate the funds provided by Schedule C to any other purpose than that of Christian Worship.'[23]

Gipps's refusal was fully endorsed by the Colonial Office. Its own interpretation of 'public worship' had been defined by Lord Stanley in 1843, when similar problems arose in New Zealand and in Van Diemen's Land, to mean Christian worship.[24] James Stephen, the permanent Under-Secretary of State, provided some guidance in the matter to Lord Lyttelton, the Secretary of State, in his minute to Gipps's despatch: 'I suppose', he wrote, 'that there can be no doubt as to the propriety of this decision?'[25] Lord Lyttelton agreed: 'I should think none.'[26] So did Gladstone, Lyttelton's successor, who eventually wrote the despatch in reply. Only five months earlier he had expressed his agreement with Gipps's intention to regard the Church Act as operative and had instructed him that it should not be tampered with 'in any wanton spirit of innovation'. The only changes he allowed were those which would give 'more complete effect to the general principle on which the Church Extension Act, and the consequent distribution of the Funds have proceeded.'[27] Moreover, until 1847 Gladstone had consistently opposed the admission of Jews to the House of Commons and had distinguished himself as a theorist of the Christian state.[28] He could not be expected to reverse the decision of the Colonial Governor. In his despatch to Gipps's successor, Sir Charles Fitz-Roy, of 4 June 1846 Gladstone gave official sanction to Gipps's refusal: 'I approve of the answer returned by Sir G. Gipps that no funds, provided by Schedule C, could legally be applied to any other purpose than that of Christian Worship.'[29]

Thus the first attempt on the part of the Jews in New South Wales to claim a share in the £30,000 set aside by the state for public worship under Schedule C, suffered defeat at the hands of the Governor. Nevertheless, Jews in the colony must have derived some consolation and a certain measure of satisfaction from the evidently favourable colonial opinion. The *Australian* even went so far as to attack Governor Gipps in a leader called 'Religious Persecution' and branded his refusal to comply with the Address of the Legislative Council 'passive persecution but of the highest order and the most dangerous kind'.[30]

Moreover, there was still some hope of a grant out of the general revenue. An amended Jewish Petition to this effect was presented by Wentworth to the Legislative Council on 2 June 1846[31] and on 15 September he moved that an Address be presented to the Governor to put £1,000 on the estimates for the synagogue and £200 annually for a Jewish minister.[32] After a short debate[33] the motion passed by a majority of 11 votes to 5. This time Robert Lowe voted against, refusing to give his assent to any grants for religion over and above the Schedule. He was however prepared as he had been in 1845 to vote for a grant to the Jewish religion out of Schedule C.

Unlike his predecessor, Sir Charles FitzRoy was conciliatory, inclined to comply as far as he could with the Legislative Council, and generous to the point of really enjoying (*pace* James Stephen) 'doing a good-natured thing'.[34] In his reply to the Address of the Legislative Council he expressed his readiness to place £1,000 on the estimates; but with regard to an annual grant of £200 for a Jewish minister he thought it his duty to refer it 'for Her Majesty's decision', 'as it would appear that this grant might lead to a permanent charge on the Revenue and moreover that it is a measure of an unusual and, as far as he is aware, of an unprecedented nature'.[35] In his despatch to Gladstone he reported that he had considered it advisable to make a grant of £1,000 for the Jewish synagogue in Sydney, 'the members of the Jewish Religion being a numerous, respectable and influential class in this community contributing largely to the Public Revenue'. Regarding the annual stipend for a Jewish minister, he left it to the consideration of the Secretary of State. He added, partly in self justification and partly to recommend it favourably: 'It was asserted in the debate upon this address that Her Majesty's Government have not objected to Legislative Aid being afforded in support of the Jewish religion in Jamaica, and the impression on my own mind is that this assertion is correct.'[36] The new Governor showed himself fully in tune with colonial opinion on this matter and did his best to assure its success in the Colonial Office.

At this point the Jews of New South Wales found themselves on the brink of religious equality; to them the unknown factor in the situation was now the attitude of the Colonial Office. They approached the Board of Deputies of British Jews for assistance. Appealing to 'the zeal you have invariably displayed for the pro-

motion of all matters tending to raise our Holy Faith in the eye of
the world' they solicited its influence with the Secretary of State
for the Colonies, Gladstone. The financial consideration that the
grant would enable them to procure a minister from England
seems to have been to them a matter of secondary importance. 'It
will be a matter of time', as they put it, and they had not even
made up their mind about it. They were however keenly aware of
the political implications of such a grant:

> if the principle be once recognised, that the Jewish Religion shall
> receive the same state support that the Christians are entitled to, it
> will give us a political standing in religious matters, and as there are
> no political distinctions with regard to our civil rights we should then
> be placed upon perfect equality with the rest of our fellow citizens.[37]

Likewise, George Moss, the Sydney correspondent of the London
Voice of Jacob, exhorted the Board of Deputies of British Jews to
fulfil its duty to 'a distant remnant of the scattered flock' and
appealed to the editor of the *Voice of Jacob* to lend his support:
'your pen and voice could not be devoted to a better and holier
cause'. Moss also stressed the political significance of the 'cause':
'the granting of it [the minister's stipend] will evince to the world
and mankind the progress of religious toleration and the good
feeling existing between a Christian Government and her Jewish
subjects.'[38]

Thus the political influence of the Board of Deputies of British
Jews in London was enlisted by the Jews of Sydney in their
struggle for equal rights.

Governor FitzRoy's despatch reached the Colonial Office in
March 1847. The full minutes available[39] make it possible to
observe how the policy of the Colonial Office on this matter was
formed.

James Stephen in his first minute of 17 March 1847 merely
objected to FitzRoy's procedure which 'deviated from the course
pointed out by his predecessor and sanctioned by the Government
here' that individual addresses should not be taken note of by the
Governor, except under special circumstances. However in his
later minute of 22 March to Benjamin Hawes, the Parliamentary
Under-Secretary, he objected in unusually strong terms to Fitz-
Roy's grant of state aid to the Jewish religion on the grounds of
principle:

> Whether it be a prejudice or not I cannot relieve myself from the
> persuasion that a Christian Country is bound to refuse support to a

Religious system the very basis of which consists in teaching that
Christianity is a deception and the most impious of frauds.

He would sooner support Mohammedanism than Judaism and
thought the reason why people generally rather favoured Judaism
was 'the utter weakness of the Jewish system and its inability to
make proselytes'. He suggested that FitzRoy's attention be called
to Gladstone's despatch of 15 June 1846 and that he be instructed
'to conform to the regulations there laid down on the subject of
supplementary votes'.

There is evidence to show that James Stephen believed in the
political equality of British-born Jews and in 1828 had given his
opinion as legal counsel to the Colonial Office that Jewish disabilities had 'no valid legal foundation' and should be classed as
'popular errors', so that the disabilities which the Jamaican Jewish
Emancipation Act of 1825 proposed to remove had 'no real existence in point of law and consequently that the Act itself is un-
necessary.'[40] It is not likely that he later changed his views as to
the *political* position of British-born Jews. But in the New South
Wales case the question of the *religious* position of the Jew had
arisen. Here Stephen, convinced as he was that 'the religion of
Jesus Christ affords the only plausible solution of the great mystery
of human life, and the only solid foundation for any lofty or con-
solatory thoughts',[41] could not help but unburden his strong feelings in a Colonial Office minute and deny the religious equality of
the Jew in a Christian state. Moreover, it was more on the grounds
of expediency than of principle that he had advocated a policy of
religious equality of the various Christian denominations in the
British colonies. Other things being equal he most probably would
have favoured 'the English or Scotch Churches'.[42]

Benjamin Hawes expressed his utter disagreement with
Stephen's views and advice. In his minute of the same day he
wrote: 'I own I do not participate in Mr. Stephen's opinions upon
this point. I should not only approve what is done but sanction
the stipend.'[43] But Benjamin Hawes had the reputation of a liberal-
radical Whig.[44] In 1841 he had come out strongly in favour of the
admission of Jews to corporate offices in England on the ground
that the state had nothing to do 'with a man's opinions', and voted
consistently in favour of Jewish emancipation.[45]

It was now left to the Secretary of State, Earl Grey, to arrive at
a policy on a matter where his two under-secretaries were in fundamental disagreement. For many years Grey had opposed Jewish

emancipation. As late as 1858 he confessed that he had found it difficult to make up his mind on the question of Jewish disabilities as there was 'much to be said on both sides' of the question: 'the arguments for and against . . . at one time appeared to me so nicely balanced, that I am not ashamed to confess it was with some difficulty I made up my mind that, on the whole, the preponderance inclined in favour of the removal of these disabilities.'[46] Undoubtedly he agreed with James Stephen in objecting to Fitz-Roy's procedure as such 'without reference to the particular object'. He seemed to waver, reluctant to express any firm opinion on the principle involved. In his minute which preceded his draft of a reply to FitzRoy he wrote:

> I do not feel the very strong objections which Mr. Stephen has expressed to the principle of a grant in support of the Jewish religion, but I am far from differing from him upon this point to the same extent as Mr. Hawes. The subject is one of great difficulty into which I do not think it advisable to enter further in a public despatch than can be avoided.[47]

Yet his despatch shows that he more or less agreed with Stephen also with regard to the principle of state aid to Jewish religion. He instructed FitzRoy to conform in future to the rule proposed by Governor Gipps regarding requests of the Legislative Council for special appropriations and not to take notice 'except in particular cases which might demand special attention'. He then proceeded to the heart of the matter and informed FitzRoy of his misgivings: 'I entertain serious doubts as to the propriety of such Grants being made at all by the Council in aid of the Jewish religion'. He conceded, however, that the will of the colonial legislature should not be vetoed indefinitely:

> If the opinion of the Council and of the Inhabitants of the Colony generally should be very strongly in favour of so wide an extension of the principle of granting assistance from the Colonial Revenue for the Religious instruction of the members of different communities, I am not prepared to instruct you to refuse your assent to such a proposal, although I should certainly regret its adoption.

But such concession should be made by way of an amendment of the colonial Church Act and 'according to some definite rule' and not by a special vote. He told FitzRoy not to accede to the Address of the Legislative Council and to refuse the grant of an annual stipend for a Jewish minister. As a parting rap on the knuckles he added: 'I should have been glad if you had not consented to make provision for the liquidation of the debt incurred in building the Synagogue.'[48]

With this despatch the position of the Colonial Office with regard to the question of the religious equality of the Jews in the Australian colonies had been clearly defined: Stanley and Gladstone had laid down that 'public worship' meant 'Christian' worship and that the Church Act had not been superseded by the Constitution Act of 1842 and should not be interfered with unless there were some weighty reasons, so that state aid to religion out of Schedule C could only be granted to Christian denominations. Grey regretted the synagogue grant and wanted no more of such special appropriations.

For Sydney Jews the disappointment was the more acute because unexpected. Their religious equality had been almost in sight and had all but vanished. Indeed the 'Report of the Committee of the Sydney Synagogue for the Year 5607' (1846–7) which purported to 'ascertain' the 'true position' of the Jewish community in New South Wales 'politically, religiously and financially', had already rejoiced in the 'political eminence' it had achieved:

> the distinct recognition of our religion by the Government of this British colony, by granting us aid from the general revenue, has affirmed the principle put forth by the British Parliament, that no man should be deprived of his political rights for his religious opinions.

It praised the 'enlightened policy' of the British government which 'has set so noble an example to the world' in 'raising the JEW (the true worshipper of ONE eternal God) to his proper place in society—that of a rational, intelligent being, invested with all the political and national privileges that belong to his fellow-countrymen and British-born subjects.'[49]

Both the language and the aspiration are unmistakably that of the *Haskalah*, the Jewish enlightenment movement of the nineteenth century, and its prose that of the congregation's talented, dedicated and impecunious honorary secretary, the emancipist George Moss. He was the colony's untiring *Maskil* or worker for *Haskalah* as founder and chairman of the Jewish Library and Hebraic Association, as editor of the ephemeral Sydney *Voice of Jacob* and Sydney correspondent of the London *Voice of Jacob*. He certainly was the moving spirit behind Sydney Jews' struggle for equality. That struggle was now connected with the emancipation of the Australian colonies from the control of the Colonial

D

Office in their internal affairs. The fateful preamble of Bourke's Church Act, Gladstone's injunction not to tamper with it, and finally the authoritative instruction of Earl Grey became for many years to come a great stumbling block in Jewish attempts to attain religious equality both in New South Wales and in Victoria.

4

The Only Grievance Removed in
New South Wales 1849-1855

The significance of Earl Grey's veto became fully apparent in August 1849 when Wentworth sought to amend the Church Act so as to include the Jewish religion under its provisions. As Wentworth insisted in the course of the debate in the Legislative Council on 28 August 1849,[1] his Church Act Extension Bill was a measure of the type Grey had stipulated in his despatch to Governor FitzRoy. Yet after Grey's censure of FitzRoy even Wentworth's proposed amendment of the Church Act could no longer command the necessary support in the Legislative Council. The colonial government had fully understood the will of its master in the Colonial Office and was determined not to antagonize him any further. Deas Thomson, the Colonial Secretary, led the opposition to Wentworth's motion and objected to it now on the ground that the Bill, if passed, would require an appropriation of money, and under clause 34 of the Constitution Act should therefore have been initiated by the Governor with the advice of the Legislative Council.[2] It must have been obvious that Grey's despatch made it very unlikely that FitzRoy could now take such an initiative. Deas Thomson certainly thought that 'they could not extend at present the provisions of the Church Act to Jews'. He declared however that 'he should be glad to see the Jews, who he believed were a highly respectable class in the community, admitted to equal privileges in this respect.'[3]

Wentworth in an effort to counterbalance the authority of the Colonial Secretary appealed to both the liberal and the religious feelings of Council members:

In some of the West Indies colonies, in Jamaica . . . in the Nether-

41

lands, in Belgium, in France, the distinctions in this respect [state aid to religion] had been swept away, and they at the antipodes of the globe, were to repudiate that policy of liberalism on these matters, which was spreading over the whole world.

Taking a leaf out of Disraeli's famous speech in the House of Commons of 1847,[4] he pleaded:

the faith which they now sought to stigmatize was the foundation on which their own worship was based. Now they would spurn from them this hoary and venerable faith—forgetting that it was their own, only in another shape. The virtues of the Christian were the virtues of the Jews—they were the virtues which the Messiah came down to teach that race—they were the virtues which proved the waters on which the Messiah marched.

Yet even Wentworth's passionate New Testament oratory could not prevail against the clear and authoritative lead given by the Colonial Secretary. When the vote was taken Wentworth's motion was defeated by 13 to 11. As could have been expected, the majority included all government members and almost all nominees.[5]

After the failure of Wentworth's Bill, Sydney Jews desisted for some years from pressing their claims. At first they may have awaited the outcome of the 1850 Petition of the Jews of Melbourne to the Secretary of State.[6] Grey's reply of 1851, though somewhat more accommodating, still made it clear that the only way in which Jewish claims to a share in state aid could be satisfied was by an amendment of the Church Act;[7] but that had been tried and had failed with the defeat of the Church Act Extension Bill of 1849. The next attempt was in 1853, when a chief rabbi to whom a comfortable salary had been promised[8] was about to arrive from England. It was decided to petition the Legislative Council again. Perhaps the knowledge that Grey had resigned from the Colonial Office raised new hopes. The Petition referred to the specific need for a chief rabbi and to the general principle that Jews as 'loyal citizens' were 'entitled to be placed upon an equality with all other Religious Denominations, consistently with their numbers.'[9]

Again Wentworth was the champion. He moved on 20 September 1853 that the Legislative Council ask the Governor-General to initiate a Bill to provide from general revenue for the payment of 'a stipend to a Minister of Religion for the congregation of persons professing the Hebrew faith in the city of Sydney.' This allowed for the requirement that the Governor must initiate money bills but Deas Thomson, who led the opposition as in 1849, thought that in the light of Grey's despatch of 1847 no 'discretion was left to the local government in the matter'. The question of a stipend to a Jewish minister could only be solved by a revision of the Church Act. But this 'opened out a very large question'. Perhaps it also signified a continuing reluctance to go in any way against Grey's old instructions. H. G. Douglas, surgeon, philosopher, humanist and a close friend of Wentworth, spoke up for the Jews and for colonial independence against Colonial Office 'dictation'; the imperial government could not object to a measure of this kind if proposed by the colonial legislature, nor should they feel bound by what Grey had said, when 'the very name of the noble lord would grate upon [their] ears'. 'Indeed they must tell Earl Grey, or any Secretary of State, that on every principle of independence, character and expediency, they would do what they thought was right, and not be dictated upon such subjects.' Relating the question of the stipend to the wider issue of Jewish emancipation in England, he took the opportunity to vent his anticlerical feelings:

> On what principle . . . did the House refuse this petty sum, when in England a great struggle was going on, to give to the Jews the full privileges possessed by their fellow Christians and which, by this time, they would have obtained, had it not been for the obstructive policy of the Bench of Bishops; it was a shame that that body could defeat the measure for the relief of the Jews.[10]

Wentworth, in the liberal tradition, referred to the general principle of religious equality according to which 'any religious class which might spring up in the colony', even Mohammedans, would be entitled to state aid. *A fortiori* the Jews, who he believed, had 'a better claim' than the Mohammedans, Christianity being 'only an emanation from the Jewish religion'. On the same ground George R. Nichols, a former editor of the radical *Australian*, a liberal and possibly of Jewish descent,[11] thought that the Bourke Church Act, as framed, was a 'mistake' and that Bourke 'originally intended that every congregation should be allowed £200'. But his liberalism would go no further than to extend state aid to the Jews, 'the original propagators of Christianity' and not to Mohammedans and pagans.

Robert Campbell, a leading Sydney merchant, Freemason and

liberal, had the distinction of bringing into array a new argument: he drew attention to the novel economic and social status Jews had achieved in New South Wales, so different from a not so distant past in the Old World:

> Fifty years ago . . . there was scarcely an instance of a Jew becoming a landed proprietor. There were weighty reasons to deter a Jew from buying land. In this colony, particularly in the city of Sydney, the names of wealthy Jews were to be found prominently amongst the most extensive purchasers of land, and this was one reason why he voted in favour of a motion which had for its object the imparting of religious instruction to the families of those who held so large a stake in the colony.

Campbell's reference to the solid stake and social status of the Jewish settlers in the colony was greeted with 'Cheers'. Yet the conservative and exclusive James Macarthur, a landed proprietor and wealthy pastoralist of somewhat older vintage, was still not convinced. He felt the question should not be dealt with 'on the commercial principles of free trade' but in accordance with a 'far higher principle', that of the Christian state: 'Christianity was part and parcel of the law of England, and that principle ought not to be violated or infringed by a hasty measure.' T. A. Murray, another pastoralist, advanced the Christian state argument and drew opposite conclusions from Campbell's thesis: 'the Jews as a body, or a sect, were the wealthiest in proportion to their numbers of the community and surely they could well afford to give a proper salary to their Rabbi'. Defenders of the Christian state responded with 'Loud cries of Hear'.

In his final plea for a positive vote, Wentworth accused the Colonial Secretary of thinking still in the terms of the 1840s and not yet in the spirit of Lord Pakington's despatch of 1852 which conceded responsible government to the colony; playing on the twin themes of colonial independence and liberalism, he exclaimed: 'Was it not too bad, on the eve of responsible government being granted to them, and when the people of England were striving to free the Jews from the barbarous restrictions of old times, that the Government should fall back on such a pretext?' When the vote was taken in the Legislative Council it resulted in a draw (14 to 14) and the revision was rejected by the casting vote of the Speaker. All government members and almost all nominee members voted against Wentworth's motion;[12] 'free' opinion in the Council was heavily for it.

Henry Parkes's liberal and 'abolitionist' *Empire*, in its comment on the adverse vote, advised the Jews to take the road to voluntaryism:

> Our friends the Jews well know that we have pleaded for their rights as firmly as we have for our own, and on the same grounds of equity too. We feel we have the right to ask them to accept our recommendation, never again to apply to the Legislature for a benevolence for their religious institutions. They will honor themselves by the abstinence.[13]

Sydney Jews, however, were of a different mind. They must have regarded it precisely as a question of their honour and status in colonial society not to be excluded from state aid. Undaunted and persistent as ever, they renewed the struggle for their inclusion into the provision of the Church Act in the following year.

Wentworth had left for England early in 1854; it was Nichols who moved on 22 August 1854 in the Legislative Council for an address to the Governor-General to initiate a Bill for a stipend to a Jewish minister out of the general revenue.[14] Nichols and all those who spoke in favour of the motion stressed the point that Jews, when pressing for a share in state aid, were not actuated 'by any merely pecuniary considerations' but by a desire to obtain 'justice and equality'. A. T. Holroyd, a humanist, doctor and farmer, pleaded against discrimination: 'He appealed to the House if in accordance with justice the Jews ought to be shut out from their fair share . . . merely because their forefathers were born in Palestine'. In answer to the Mohammedan scare, put up by the Colonial Secretary and others, he declared that should Mohammedans 'require State support for their Mollahs, he would rejoice to see their minarets adorn the city'. The fact that the Solicitor-General, W. M. Manning, spoke in support of the motion showed that the matter was no longer regarded as a government question. But Deas Thomson, the Colonial Secretary, renewed his opposition and suggested that the object of Jewish equality would not be achieved if Jews were given aid out of the general revenue, while the Christian denominations received it under Schedule C.

In the lengthy debate in the Legislative Council only two speakers—Charles Cowper and James Martin—opposed the motion on the ground of principle. Cowper, as consistent as ever, was opposed to state aid altogether, unless the state supported 'one established Church' exclusively, i.e. *the* 'Established Church'. Yet he thought that under the system of state aid, to which he was opposed, Jews were entitled to equality with others and that this had been the original intention of Bourke's Church Act:

> He believed that the original petition upon which the Bill of Sir Richard Bourke was founded did not contain the words in the Act . . . as to the advancement of Christian religion and he believed that the draft of that Act which was originally drawn up, did not contain these words and was intended to make the grant unlimited in its action.[15]

If Cowper opposed the motion because he believed in an established church and objected to state aid to other churches, James Martin, the colony's Edmund Burke, fought it with weapons borrowed from the Christian-state champions in England. Though Martin's polished eloquence could not sway the vote, his views deserve fuller treatment since they must have driven home to members in the Legislative Council, and to Jews and their friends outside, that the question at issue was nothing less than Jewish emancipation within the Australian context.

He began by attacking the Solicitor-General for having advanced the view that Christianity and Judaism were substantially alike, and remarked that 'such an opinion obtained very little currency' in the English Parliament. Holding up the English constitution which 'had never yet recognized any other religion than that of Christ' as the model, he exclaimed:

> why should they in this colony take upon themselves to violate in spirit and practice the great constitutional principle of the parent country? . . . the whole of the laws of England were based upon Christianity.

The question at issue as he saw it was:

> whether they would allow a people who professed themselves to be a distinct and separate nation, to step in and share with them those privileges which were intended for British subjects alone and which were peculiar to the Christian auspices under which they lived.

Pursuing the argument to its conclusion, oblivious of the realities of colonial society, he declared:

> The Jews had always avowed themselves a distinct and separate race and he had always looked upon them as such. It was not incompatible with their isolated character that they should emigrate to a country like this, and to remain in it so long as it was convenient and suited their worldly interests.

He would extend to Jews in civil and political matters all the rights
and privileges which were enjoyed by Christians under the British
government, as in the mother country, but 'the Imperial Parliament had never yet recognized in any shape whatever the religious
position of the Jew.' As a case in point he referred to the fact that
'the very last bill which was introduced into Parliament for the
purpose of removing the religious disabilities of the Jews was
thrown out by a majority of four'.[16] He finally called upon members not to let themselves be swayed by their sympathies for the
Jews who 'in this colony had by their numerous acts of charity
and their general usefulness as members of the community secured
to themselves many friends' but to remain true to the principle
which they had 'all along' upheld.[17]

Henry Parkes, the colony's outstanding democrat, abolitionist
and 'unchanging friend' of Jacob Levi Montefiore, championed the
Jewish cause *and* used it in his argument against state aid: his
'one great objection' was that it drove the government and the
legislature into 'an act of inconsistency', either to support a religion
which they did not profess or to 'commit an act of political injustice' for, politically considered, there could be no doubt but that
the Jews had as much right as any other body to the support of the
state, as they contributed equally to the burdens of the state.
Therefore, as long as the state lent its aid to various bodies of
religionists, 'he should vote for the support to all who, on political
grounds, could show a fair and equitable claim to its exercise.'[18]

If Martin referred to English precedent as binding, and reflected
more than anything the views and fears of conservative Englishmen when faced with the Jewish emancipation movement in
England, George Nichols like Wentworth before him appears
more as the spokesman for colonial independence and of emancipation from English tutelage. In his final appeal he taxed the
Colonial Secretary with subservience to the Colonial Office:

> It was probable that he bore in mind the rap over the knuckles which
> the tyrant of the Colonial Office, Lord Grey, gave a former Executive
> for granting the sum of £1,000 to the Jews . . . The day when that
> occurred was passed and was not likely soon to return.

He then countered Martin's arguments: 'He would ask whether the
Jews in this country were not the bona fide settlers of the land,
whether they had not a very large amount of capital at stake in the
general prosperity of the country?' Nichols ended on a note of liberal optimism and an implied censure of England's prejudices: 'he

had great hope that he would yet live to see a young Australian Jew of high intellectual attainments occupying a seat in that House, notwithstanding any disabilities which may at present stay in the way.' That Nichols's views and remarks were more in tune with colonial opinion, and reflected more faithfully colonial reality than those of Martin, can be gauged from the 'Cheers' with which they were greeted, and from the vote. His motion succeeded by a two-thirds majority (20 to 10), four government members voting in favour.[19]

There were hurdles still: the Governor-General, and above all the Colonial Office on whose attitudes so much depended. Governor-General FitzRoy in his reply to the Address of the Legislative Council of 21 September informed it that he could not comply with the Address finding himself 'precluded by the terms of the Secretary of State's Despatch of 13th April, 1847'. On the motion of G. R. Nichols on 3 October the Governor-General was asked to forward the Address of the Legislative Council of 22 August to the Secretary of State together with his favourable recommendation.[20]

FitzRoy in his despatch of 18 October 1854 which accompanied the Address of the Legislative Council briefly explained that he had refused because he felt himself bound by Earl Grey's despatch of 1847. He concluded on a dry, non-committal note and with some touch of concealed rancour: 'In forwarding these Addresses for your consideration, in compliance with the request of the Legislative Council, I do not feel myself at liberty to express my opinion any further in the matter.'[21] When this despatch was received in the Colonial Office on 25 January 1855 it seems to have caused some headaches.[22] Gordon Gairdner, the Senior Clerk, in his minute to Herman Merivale, the Permanent Under-Secretary, thought that it involved 'a question of principle and one of some delicacy and importance', and that it was presented 'very much in the same way' as in FitzRoy's despatch of 1846. He suggested that the minutes on that despatch be referred to as well as 'Lord Grey's instruction which was founded on those minutes'. Herman Merivale in his minute to Frederic Peel, the Parliamentary Under-Secretary, conceded that the minutes were 'important,' but consistent with views he had expressed in lectures at the University of Oxford,[23] he added: 'for my own part I regard this as wholly a question for the local legislature, and should act accordingly.' He thought it was 'unfortunate' that on a matter which is 'so very likely to excite public attention and feeling' the Governor 'has not thought proper to give us either publicly or confidentially more information', and asked that a search be made in the colonial newspapers. Gairdner then reported that Nichols's motion had been passed by 20 to 10 votes, that the Colonial Secretary had opposed it, but four government officers voted for it. 'It seems therefore to have been left an open question with the Government officers.' Gairdner then suggested that this problem 'be reserved for Lord John Russell's consideration'.

Russell, the chief champion of Jewish emancipation in England, author of many a 'Jew Bill' *and* advocate of responsible government for the colonies, had no difficulty in concurring with the opinion of his Permanent Under-Secretary, 'a staunch liberal',[24] and in arriving at a decision. He commented: 'I agree with Mr. Merivale that this is wholly a question for the local legislature. Instruct Gov. Denison to comply with the Address.'[25]

Russell's despatch to the new Governor-General, William Denison, brief as it was, marked a drastic change in the policy of the Colonial Office with regard to the question of state aid to the Jewish religion. Referring to FitzRoy's query, he wrote: 'that question Sir Charles FitzRoy had considered himself prevented by his previous instructions from entertaining, but I regard it as one wholly for the decision of the local legislature.' He instructed him in unambiguous terms: 'it will be desirable that you should comply with the Address of the Council *unless special circumstances should induce you to think it unadvisable. In that case you will state the reasons for not complying with the Address.*'[26]

Thus, by Russell's unequivocal instructions, the veto of the Colonial Office of James Stephen's and Earl Grey's days had been lifted and the struggle for Jewish religious equality in New South Wales ended in victory. Denison immediately complied with instructions and put £200 on the estimates for 1856 as a stipend for a Jewish minister.[27]

One can well imagine the rejoicing of the Jewish community in New South Wales, after ten years of struggle. In the annual report for 1854–5 we see the congregational leaders congratulating themselves on their achievement and underlining its significance: 'This will place us upon an equal footing with members of the Christian Faith and remains the sole grievance we were labouring under in this colony.'[28] At a special meeting they decided to present G. R. Nichols with a piece of plate in recognition of his advocacy of their rights and as an expression of gratitude to the Legislative Council and the Governor. In their letter of thanks to Nichols they stressed that they had been fighting for a principle:

> by the recognition of their claim to a portion of the funds set apart for Public Worship by the Governor and Legislative Council, the only grievance under which the Hebrews of this colony laboured had been removed and they consider this as a great triumph of the cause of civil and religious equality by securing to them their rights of citizens irrespective of their religious beliefs.[29]

Nichols agreed that the 'high cause of religious equality' had been vindicated and that the struggle they had been waging was for a principle:

> I am well aware that your only intention was to place yourselves upon an equal footing with other sects whose claims were recognised by the Government of this colony through the Legislative Council so as thereby to establish those rights to which you are justly entitled.[30]

Looking back after a century it may appear as if a minor inequity had been somewhat inflated, through those ten years, by people who from the beginning of Jewish settlement in New South Wales had enjoyed in practice all the civil and political rights of their Christian fellow-settlers. All they could complain about was that their minister did not receive a government stipend, whereas all Christian ministers were entitled to such a stipend and those who wished did receive one. Even this inequity was not the fault of colonial society or of the colonial government. In 1846 both had done their best, by granting £1,000 for a synagogue, to put the Jewish congregation on an equal footing with other congregations, and they had gone as far as they could to secure an annual stipend for the Jewish minister. It was chiefly the veto of the Colonial Office which had prevented the colonial legislature and the Governor from including the Jewish religion in the provisions of state aid to religion. If there were a number of colonial spokesmen who disputed the Jewish claim to religious equality on the grounds of principle, some like James Macarthur and T. A. Murray did so in a half-hearted way, whereas others, like James Martin or 'Christianus' before him, seem to represent borrowings from a very different situation than that existing in the colony.

However, our Jewish settlers too had come from a different situation, that of the old country, and had brought with them a long memory of insecurity and discrimination which was kept alive by connections with Jews abroad, and by immigration. Though in practice they enjoyed equal rights and a relatively high social status, yet there was no official declaration or legal enactment which confirmed their *de facto* position and assured them of their equal rights. The granting of state aid to their religion was to take the place of such a declaration. The numerous difficulties they encountered on the way must have increased their sensitiveness and determination to overcome them. Living in a liberal age and sharing in its belief that all inequalities and injustices could be removed by the magic wand of legislation, their coveted aim was confirmation of their emancipation by the colonial legislature.

During what remained of the 1850s in New South Wales, the achievement of 1854 and 1855 was consolidated. In October 1854 Saul Samuel, a prominent leader of the congregation, was elected to the Legislative Council, and in 1856 Jacob Levi Montefiore, merchant, financier and man of learning, was appointed to the Upper Chamber of the New Legislative Council, i.e. before Jews in England were admitted to the House of Commons. However, the rumour spread before Samuel's election that he would be unable to take his seat since he could not as a Jew take the prescribed oath of office, shows that the Jewish position was still somewhat ambiguous. Samuel thought it necessary to counter such rumours:

> a report had been circulated that because he was of the Jewish faith, he would not conform to the oath required by the law, prior to taking his seat in the house. But in New South Wales he was happy to say that such was not the fact. The oath was purely an oath of allegiance and was not, as in England, based upon an exclusive or sectarian prejudice.[31]

Two minor complications remained. Sticklers could note that the aid received from 1855 to 1859 came from supplementary grants rather than (with perfect Christian equivalence) from Schedule C. And during the debate on the Oath of Office Simplifying Bill in 1856 it transpired that Jews had to be exempted from the objectionable part of the oath of abjuration, 'upon the true faith of a Christian'. As J. H. Plunkett, the mover of the Bill, observed, 'No gentleman of the Jewish persuasion could ever act as a magistrate were it not that the present Chief Justice [Alfred Stephen] took upon himself the responsibility of dispensing with it.'[32] At the second reading of the Bill on 11 November Plunkett referred specifically to the recent case of Saul Samuel when 'the exclusive part of the oath had been dispensed with in favour of a member of the Jewish persuasion who was a credit to that House'.[33] With the pass-

ing of this Act,[34] whatever ambiguity had remained as to the position of the Jew in New South Wales had been officially removed.
Jews and Catholics were now in the same position as Protestants.
When called upon to deliver an oath of office they delivered the
same oath.

One can sense their feelings of satisfaction and pride in their
own achievement in the way in which Sydney Jews reacted three
years later to news of the Jews' Relief Act of 1858 and the admission of the first Jew, Baron Lionel Rothschild, to the British House
of Commons. At the public meeting at which Sydney Jews com-
memorated the decisive act in the achievement of Jewish political
equality in England, they referred to it as a welcome 'concession'
only and contrasted it with their own position of full equality in
New South Wales.[35] As Saul Samuel put it: 'the concession made
was only the insertion of the small end of the wedge, for the resolution of Parliament declaratory of the civil rights of the Jews was
not yet comprehensive and affirmative.' Moss Israel could not see
why they should express their gratitude to the government and
parliament of England for this small instalment of religious liberty:
'they should rather congratulate Englishmen upon having come to
a true sense of justice . . . and urge them on to enlarge that liberty
and thereby wipe out . . . all that remained as the result of those
bigoted ideas which had disgraced English legislation.' In the
letter sent to Lionel Rothschild they congratulated him upon
having taken

> his seat in the British House of Commons and having been practically
> the instrument through whom the British Jews have obtained their
> political rights, rights which happily we already enjoy through the
> liberality of the legislature of our Colony.[36]

Yet only two months after they had celebrated the Jews' Relief
Act, Sydney Jews suffered an unexpected setback when the stipend
for a Jewish minister was discontinued. That stipend, granted since
1855, came from a supplementary grant of £14,025 which had
been voted over and above Schedule C.[37] In December 1858 the
voluntaryists managed to do away with the supplementary grant
as the first step towards the general abolition of state aid to religion.
Thus the source of the Jewish minister's stipend was abolished.[38]

How sensitive and jealous Sydney Jews were in the matter of
state aid can be gauged from the speed with which they acted 'to
maintain their political position in this colony'.[39] Only two days
after the abolition, a general meeting of Sydney Jews protested

against their exclusion from state aid and petitioned the Legislative Assembly:

> in depriving them of the Stipend previously granted towards the support of a Jewish Minister your Petitioners would be the only religious class excluded from State aid—clergymen of other denominations still receiving partial support as provided in Schedule C—whereby a precedent would be created destructive of that religious equality which has been hitherto happily recognised in your Honourable House.[40]

The long struggle for equality was to end in anticlimax. In 1859 the Sydney Jewish community split from top to bottom on a very sensitive religious issue when the Acting Minister, the Rev. Morrice R. Cohen, refused to perform the full rite of circumcision on a newborn boy whose mother's Jewish credentials he questioned. One party, that of the future secessionists who were led by the stalwarts P. J. Cohen and his brother Samuel, angrily denounced the unbending zeal of the Minister as a 'Jewish Inquisition' born of malice, and demanded his dismissal. The other party, the future 'old congregationalists', would have nothing of that but testified to 'the zeal and efficiency displayed by the Rev. M. R. Cohen' and proposed his promotion and the 'augmentation of his present stipend'. The party worsted in the conflict seceded and formed itself into a new (Macquarie Street) congregation, appointed its own minister and refused to have anything to do with the old (York Street) congregation, even on so vital a matter of common concern as state aid to religion.[41]

Thus it came about that in January 1860 the Legislative Council was called upon to adjudicate between two rival Jewish Petitions, that of the (Macquarie Street) secessionists presented by Fawcett which asked for £200 state aid out of the supplementary estimates and the Counter-petition of the York Street congregationalists presented by Saul Samuel which prayed that 'the House would not assent to the motion of Mr. Fawcett for a state allowance of £200 to the Jewish minister'.[42] The old congregationalists said they were opposed to state aid to religion altogether, certainly to any increase in state aid over and above Schedule C. Still, so long as state aid was continued by the £28,000 set aside by the Constitution Act for aid to public worship, 'they assert the right of the Jewish community to a portion of that sum'.[43] The secessionists too were in favour of the abolition of state aid to religion (and had signed the Jewish Petition of 1858) but they were also very eager to receive state aid for their minister, even if this meant an augmentation of state aid from the supplementary estimates, something abolitionists very much disapproved of. The secessionist Petition was then not so much another instance in the Jewish struggle for equality as a public assertion of their independence from the old congregation.

The whole incident provides some insight into the Jewish attitude to state aid. While Jews in tune with colonial liberal opinion were generally against it, they felt more strongly for religious equality expressed in an equal share in state aid as long as it was disbursed. While the old congregationalists seem to have agreed to receive a nine months' salary for their minister as compensation for the abolition of the supplementary grant *and* in anticipation of the abolition of state aid altogether, the secessionists 'went it alone' and applied for a grant from the supplementary estimates, and thus invited the censure of abolitionists like Lang who feared the Jewish Petition would be used 'as a fetch to strengthen the hands of those who were endeavouring to perpetuate the system of state-aid'.[44] As could have been expected, Fawcett's motion was heavily defeated by 22 votes to 9.[45] For the next three years neither Jewish congregation received state aid for their ministers.

All aid to religion in New South Wales ended with the victory of the voluntary principle in religion in 1862. That ended the last Jewish grievance, and made Jewish religious equality complete.

5

Jews in a Christian State: Van Diemen's Land under Sir John Franklin

While in New South Wales the fate of Jewish religious equality depended largely on the policy of the Colonial Office in distant London, in Van Diemen's Land it was decided by a Colonial Governor who discriminated against organized Jewish religion as a matter of principle. Sir John Franklin's government was an extreme case of the Christian state in action.

Jews in Van Diemen's Land were heard of for the first time when in May 1828 Barnard Walford, an emancipist baker, applied on behalf of a small group in Hobart to Lieutenant-Governor George Arthur for a grant of land for a Jewish cemetery. Arthur granted them a substantial piece of land and seems to have assured the petitioners of his good will and intention to assist all religious denominations. Whereupon a grateful and somewhat ignorant Walford promised to 'convey to our revered and highly respected priest [*sic*] in England' how well he and his fellow-Jews had been treated by the Governor.[1]

However, when in September 1832 a small group of Jews in Launceston applied for a grant of land for a cemetery, Arthur let them know that 'further allocation of Land cannot be granted, but any spot required will be put up for sale'.[2] Arthur's reasons for this qualified refusal are not known for certain. His answer seems to suggest that he acted in accordance with the Ripon Regulations of 1831 which did away with free land grants;[3] and he may have regarded the nine Launceston Jews as too few to justify a special and now rather exceptional grant.[4]

Some Jewish meetings are said to have been held from 1830 in the private residence of the enterprising, wealthy and unsavoury emancipist Judah Solomon in Hobart, and a Jewish philanthropic

55

E

society is believed to have been in existence there from 1836,[5] but the small group of Jewish emancipist shopkeepers, innkeepers and traders which included Judah and his brother Joseph Solomon and the notorious 'Ikey' Solomon, the prototype of Dickens's Fagin, seems to have been singlemindedly concerned with commerce, including some shady dealing and some usury. The uncharitable *Colonial Times* of 18 December 1832 denounced Hobart Jews as 'beardless Shylocks . . . who like incubuses have fastened on [the colony] or who rather as vultures have preyed [on] its vitals'.[6]

The initiative to found a Hebrew congregation proper did not come from the 'beardless Shylocks' but from some young free Jewish settlers including Jacob Frankel (who had qualified for the Jewish ministry), Edward Isaacs and Henry Horwitz who arrived in Hobart from London early in 1842 and promptly prodded into action such well-established Jewish settlers as the prosperous merchant Louis Nathan (he and his family arrived in 1834), the aristocratic and aloof David R. Furtado (a business partner of J. B. Montefiore) and the very observant Isaac Friedman (who came from Sydney in 1840). When the congregation was formally established Louis Nathan was elected president and Judah Solomon treasurer.[7] The honorary secretary was the well-educated and cultured Phineas Moss who worked as Chief Clerk of the Registrar in the Probation Department.[8] While Nathan was for many years the respectable and permanent head of the congregation and Judah Solomon its financial benefactor (among other things he donated the land on which the synagogue was erected), Phineas Moss became the intellectual driving force in its life and struggle for equal rights.

The first clash with the colonial administration occurred in September 1842 when the newly founded congregation applied to Captain Matthew Forster, Chief Police-Magistrate and Probation Director, to allow Jewish convicts to attend services on the Day of Atonement and to let the Jewish convict Caspar be present at the burial of his son.[9] Captain Forster, true to his form as the 'Aga of the Janissaries of Little Botany Bay',[10] refused both applications. Hobart Jews applied then to the Lieutenant-Governor, Sir John Franklin, who may have been unaware of Captain Forster's refusal when he replied that 'on Captain Forster's recommendation he should be happy to accede to their request'. They applied a second time and when Captain Forster refused again, they would not persist.[11] They may have construed Franklin's reply as a diplomatic evasion or as a sign of his notorious weakness when dealing with

Captain Forster; in either case there was little they could do while Forster remained in charge of the convict establishment. They interpreted the rebuff as an official religious discrimination, and communicated their grievance to the local press and to the *Voice of Jacob* in London.[12] The local papers were friendly.[13] Even the *Hobart Town Advertiser*, which was by no means hostile to Franklin's government, had championed the cause of the Jewish convicts against Forster and Franklin.

By 1843 the number of free Jewish settlers in Van Diemen's Land had grown to some three hundred,[14] apart from an unknown but 'considerable number' of Jewish convicts,[15] and both Hobart and Launceston Jews decided to build synagogues. Though times were bad and Van Diemen's Land in the throes of a deep depression,[16] Jews in Hobart *and* their Christian friends[17] soon donated some £500 to the building fund. They may have felt that both their numbers and the funds in hand entitled them to state aid. They petitioned the Lieutenant-Governor, 'soliciting aid from the Government funds'.[18] They were promptly informed 'the principle of the Church Act is not sufficiently comprehensive to sanction the giving of the Aid applied for'.[19]

There can hardly be any doubt that, in this refusal, Franklin did act with the advice of his Executive Council[20] and in accordance with the letter and spirit of the Van Diemen's Land Church Act of 1837.[21] He was its author—it was known as the 'Franklin Church Act'—and he had modelled it on the Bourke Church Act which made provision for Christian denominations only.[22] In Sydney the Constitution Act of 1842 cast some doubt on the validity of the Christian preamble of the Bourke Church Act, but the doubt did not extend to Van Diemen's Land. The political and ecclesiastical arrangements of this penal colony remained unaffected by the Constitution Act.[23]

In Launceston Jews applied not for state aid but merely for a grant of land for a synagogue and a cemetery. Franklin refused this also. The story of this refusal is well worth telling as the only clear-cut case in the Australian colonies of religious discrimination against a group of Jewish settlers as a matter of principle. Moreover, the Colonial Office under Lord Stanley, by upholding Franklin's decision in the Launceston case, established an interpretation of the formula 'Public Worship' which included the Christian religion undefined, but excluded the Jewish religion. Thus Franklin's refusal helped to shape Colonial Office policy.

In Launceston a small group of Jewish settlers is said to have

formed a Benevolent Society in 1838 to assist the Jewish poor.[24]
A proper Hebrew congregation, headed by the old settler Henry
Davis and the more recent arrivals Benjamin Francis, a prosperous
emancipist, and David Benjamin, a young respectable merchant,
was established only in 1842, and its first major activity was the
collection of funds for the building of a synagogue. Early in 1843
some £400 had been collected and an application for land for
synagogue and cemetery was made to the Lieutenant-Governor.
To strengthen their case the Launceston Jews told Franklin that
'their number has of late greatly increased in the Northern Division of this Island and that there is every probability of an acces-
sion to their number yearly by Emigration and other means'.[25] He
refused their request point blank and when asked whether he
would recommend a Petition which they intended to forward to
the Secretary of State for the Colonies, he made it clear he would
not.[26]

The press was as indignant as the Jews. The notoriously anti-
Franklin *Cornwall Chronicle* embraced the cause with gusto, accused Franklin of 'illiberal prejudice', and branded his treatment
of the 'now numerous and respectable professors of the Jewish
religion' as 'illiberal in the extreme'. By contrast, it praised his predecessor, Governor Arthur, who had granted land to the Jews of
Hobart though they were then 'much less numerous than those
resident in Launceston and its vicinity at this time', and declared
that 'the treatment perpetrated on the body of Jews by his Excellency Sir John Franklin, has created a universal feeling of dissatis-
faction and we may add disgust'.[27]

The rival paper, the *Launceston Examiner*, though more re-
strained in its censure of the Governor, deplored that 'Sir John
Franklin whose character is usually exempt from the blemish of
bigotry, should allow an illiberal prejudice to obstruct the success
of the applicants'. The state as such had nothing to do with 'dog-
matical theology', and 'the suppression of error or the propaga-
tion of truth' were outside its competence. The state recognized
ministers of religion and assisted them financially merely as
'teachers of a people' and not because of 'the abstract merits of their
several creeds'. Jews should participate 'in the privileges conceded
to others' on the ground of justice, which required 'the impartial
distribution of advantages to all who equally contribute to the
funds of the state'; the *Examiner* called upon the government to
'adopt as a maxim to give to all or to give to none'.[28]

In the knowledge that Governors Arthur, Bourke and Gipps had granted land for cemeteries and a synagogue, the Launceston Jews decided late in May 1843 to petition the Secretary of State, Lord Stanley.[29] The petitioners described themselves as 'merchants, traders, and others, members of the Jewish persuasion . . . subjects of Great Britain resident at Launceston'. They complained of Franklin's treatment of them and accused him of anti-Jewish prejudice:

> his Excellency Sir John Franklin evinced the most marked hostility towards the attainment of the object of their petition; so evident as to call forth the animadversions of each member of the deputation; and which hostility your lordship's petitioners can attribute to no other source than that of a feeling personally inimical to the religion which the petitioners profess; and which they never anticipated would be so strongly displayed by any individual holding the high and responsible position of Her Majesty's representative.

Referring to precedents of grants of land to Jewish religious bodies in Hobart and in New South Wales and to some smaller Christian sects in Van Diemen's Land, the petitioners urged that

> as British subjects, permitted the free exercise in common with others to their own particular tenets, they are equally entitled . . . to the assistance and countenance of the government, and to receive the same consideration, and be placed on an equal footing in every respect as they are.

Finally, they 'solicit respectfully but urgently' that the Secretary of State 'will be pleased to direct the grant to them of a piece of land in the township of Launceston whereon to erect a synagogue and form a cemetery for the interment of their dead.'

At the same time they asked Sir Moses Montefiore, President of the Board of Deputies of British Jews, to intervene on their behalf with the Colonial Office.[30] As the London *Voice of Jacob* reported, 'Sir Moses . . . expressed his fullest concurrence in the prayer of the Petition and promised that it should receive his utmost support.'[31]

The Petition was published in a number of Van Diemen's Land newspapers. Their comments show that the bitterness of Launceston Jews was well understood. The *Launceston Examiner* called the Petition 'a very compromising state paper' which 'will require some explanation' from the Governor. Referring to the 'language' of the petitioners, it excused it as that of 'persons who feel both insulted and injured', though it believed it unlikely that on the part of Sir John Franklin actual 'discourtesy was intended'. Here, the sensitiveness of the petitioners, the result of eighteen centuries when they had 'to suffer much from the rude and barbarous', should be taken into account.[32] A few days later, the same paper gave pointed notice to the news that in New South Wales 'Sir George Gipps has granted a burying ground to the Jews in Port Phillip'.[33] *Murray's Review* also printed the Petition, expressed its ᶠᵘllest agreement with its demands and called it 'unanswerable'.[34] The *Launceston Advertiser* urged the Jews' right to equality and exclaimed: 'the spirit of illiberality which would exclude the Jews from a participation in the common rights of mankind is despicable in the extreme'.[35] It criticized the somewhat aggressive tone of the Petition, and described its style as 'impolitic and calculated to defeat its object'. But the 'impolitic language' may have been calculated to discredit further the unpopular Governor by suggesting that he had acted from personal prejudice.

Yet Sir John Franklin's refusal to grant land to the Jews of Launceston was dictated not so much by prejudice against Jews and their religion as by his firm and uncompromising belief in a 'Christian state'. He was an evangelical Christian known for his fervent piety and was a Tory.[36] He seems to have held views on the position of Jews in a Christian state similar to those of his mentor and friend, Dr Thomas Arnold of Rugby.[37] Franklin was rather latitudinarian in his relations with and treatment of the various Christian denominations in the colony,[38] but, like Arnold's, Franklin's latitudinarianism was for Christians only.

In his despatch to Stanley, which accompanied the Petition of the Jews of Launceston to the Secretary of State, Franklin gave the reasons why he had refused to grant land to them.[39] In the first place, Launceston Jews were 'by no means numerous'. He would not consider them 'in point of numbers entitled to so considerable indulgence as a Grant of Land', even if this were 'upon principle proper'. He then made it clear that the question of numbers was of secondary importance to him and that his decision was based on colonial law and on principle:

> by the Acts of Council which provide for the erection of Places of Divine Worship the Jews are excluded from all participation in the assistance granted by the Public for that purpose, and whatever claims the Members of their persuasion may have to an equality in Civil rights, and to that Protection which the Government is desirous to extend alike to all Her Majesty's subjects, I have not felt myself justified in countenancing and propagating at the Public Expense a religion essentially hostile to that of Christ, until I shall be honoured by your Lordship's instructions upon the subject.

The Franklin Church Act of 1837, like the Bourke Church Act of 1836, made no reference to land grants. The Christian preamble of his Church Act had not prevented Sir Richard Bourke from promising a grant of land for a synagogue in Sydney, before his departure from New South Wales, nor his successor Sir George Gipps from granting that land in 1840 or from making grants of land to the small Jewish congregation of Port Phillip for a cemetery in 1843 and for a synagogue in 1844. It seems therefore that Franklin's interpretation of the colonial Church Building Acts as excluding the Jewish religion not merely from financial assistance, but even from land grants, was due to his belief in his responsibilities as governor of a Christian colony.

Referring to that part of the Petition which charged him with prejudice, Franklin assured the Secretary of State that, though he was 'certainly of opinion' that the petitioners' object 'cannot be obtained at the expense or through the intervention of the Government', yet he was 'ever influenced by the same earnest desire of seeing every class of Her Majesty's subjects advance in prosperity and wealth, and by those enlarged principles of toleration which form so prominent a part of the British Constitution.'

Finally, he mentioned 'a somewhat similar application' of the Jews of Hobart which, with the advice of the Executive Council, he had 'in like manner been compelled to decline'.[40] Franklin thus lumped together the Launceston application for a land grant with the Hobart request for state aid. While in the Hobart case his refusal was borne out by the Church Act, this was not necessarily so with regard to the Launceston case. Here, in the light of his despatch to Stanley, it appears that Franklin's grim Christian faith[41] was responsible for a policy which differed so markedly from the practice of other Australian governors.

Franklin was already unpopular in the colony. The petitioners may have hoped that he was also unpopular with the Secretary of State for the Colonies. It was public knowledge that Stanley had firmly refused to sanction Franklin's dismissal of John Montagu, the Colonial Secretary of Van Diemen's Land, and rumours were spreading in the colony about the impending recall of the Governor.[42] Moreover, they may have shared the hope of the *Launceston Examiner* that Lord Stanley, 'however disposed to toryism' was 'too keen a politician to be ostentatious of unprofitable intolerance', and not likely to miss an opportunity to 'display liberality', for reasons of expediency, though not of conviction.[43] In the event, as we shall see, Stanley did no such thing, but upheld Franklin's decision.

Franklin's despatch of 14 June 1843 was received in the Colonial Office as late as 12 December 1843. A copy of the Launceston Jewish Petition had reached the Colonial Office almost four weeks earlier, enclosed in a letter in which Sir Moses Montefiore asked Lord Stanley for an interview, referring to precedents of colonial land grants to Jewish congregations, and remarked that he found it difficult to understand 'why in this particular instance the same indulgence should not be accorded as in the several instances adverted to by the Petitioners.' Since Franklin's despatch was not yet on hand, his successor in Van Diemen's Land, Sir John Eardley-Wilmot, was asked to report on the matter.[44] Eventually Franklin's despatch arrived and his side of the story could be considered. The Colonial Office minutes enable us to see how Stanley arrived at his decision to uphold Franklin's refusal.[45]

This was not the first time that the Colonial Office had considered the question of colonial land grants for Jewish religious purposes. Only two months before, in October 1843, a despatch had arrived from Willoughby Shortland, Acting Governor of New Zealand, in which he had reported that the Jews of Wellington had applied to him for grants of land for a cemetery and a synagogue. He had granted them land for a cemetery but not for the synagogue, informing them that for the latter he had no authority 'without the express sanction of Her Majesty's Government'—'under my present instructions I do not feel justified in alienating Land to the Professors of any but a Christian Creed'.[46] James Stephen, the Permanent Under-Secretary who minuted Shortland's despatch, seems to have been wary of expressing an opinion: 'The question to which this Despatch refers is one which touches a very broad general principle respecting which I can have nothing to offer with which your Lordship is not already familiar.'[47] Thus unhelped, Stanley tried to ascertain what Shortland's 'existing instructions' were and whether the case was covered by the Land Sales Acts.[48] He was told by Gordon Gairdner, the Senior Clerk, that the relevant section of the Land Sales Act 'would cover either case'. It referred to 'such lands as may be required as the sites of places of Public Worship or as places for the interment of the Dead.' For a burial grant Gairdner thought that 'the discretion of the Governor was left unfettered'. As to what the 'instructions' were under which Shortland had acted, Gairdner reported that under the system of state aid in operation in the Australian colonies and in New Zealand, 'the aid of Government is confined to the various denominations of Christians . . . but there was no express prohibition against any such grant to the Jews.'[49]

All told, Gairdner's advice left Stanley free to decide the question either way. We may assume then that his eventual decision, other things being equal, was influenced by his view of that 'very broad general principle' with which, on the testimony of the erudite Stephen, he was so familiar. Indeed, Stanley was known as one of the 'bitterest and most uncompromising foes' of Jewish emancipation in England[50] and played a leading role in the opposition to the admission of 'the Jews as members of a Christian Legislature' until the very passing of the Jews' Relief Act in 1858.[51] He told Captain Robert Fitzroy, the Lieutenant-Governor of New Zealand, that he refused to comply with the Wellington Jewish application.[52] Franklin's despatch from Van Diemen's Land was minuted by T. W. C. Murdoch, Clerk in the Colonial Office.[53] Murdoch observed that Franklin had arrived at his decision by reference to the Van Diemen's Land Church Building Acts which applied 'only to the Christian Religion', but that under the Imperial Land Sales Act which referred to 'Places of Public Worship', 'the answer . . . is not so simple'. Murdoch reminded Stanley that in the New Zealand case a cemetery had been granted but a synagogue was refused. He added: 'This you approved thereby putting on the expression "Public Worship" a construction that the Christian Religion is intended.' To this, he 'would adhere'. He expressed the opinion that 'The Grant of Burial Ground would be within the rule.' Stanley however took no notice of the distinction which Murdoch had made between land for a cemetery and land for a synagogue and remarked: 'I think Sir J. Franklin is borne out in his refusal by the terms of the Colonial Laws and I'll so inform Sir M. Montefiore.'[54]

He had no reason to reverse Franklin's decision. To do so and thus further to humiliate the ex-Governor in public would have required that he disagreed with him as to the principle on which he had acted. He did not disagree: both Franklin and Stanley were firm believers in a Christian state. So was Eardley-Wilmot, who also voted in the House of Commons against Jewish emancipation.[55] His note to Stanley supported Franklin and agreed with Stanley's and Franklin's views of colonial law, and of the Christian state. Urging that the Launceston Jewish petitioners had no case, Eardley-Wilmot declared:

Christianity being part and parcel of the law of England, those who profess themselves Christians are within the Law and its advantages; and ought to, and actually do, receive every Encouragement consistent with the safety of the Church Establishment. Whereas the Jews denying Christianity, cannot be said to have any title or right to a similar indulgence.

If they were nevertheless given land in Launceston it should 'be done solely on the ground of assisting all subjects of Her Majesty equally with a mark of Royal favour and not on religious grounds.'[56]

Between the two very Christian governors and the Christian Secretary of State, Launceston Jews were left without a land grant and had to buy the land upon which their synagogue was built. As usual, the material cost was only a minor part of their continuing grievance; they were more concerned with the inequality it symbolized. In the convict settlement of Van Diemen's Land, they were told in so many words that they were not equal with others because they happened to live in a Christian state. Or rather, *under* one; they had no cause to complain of their Christian fellow-colonists, who expressed their sympathy by generous contributions to the Hobart and Launceston synagogues[57] and by the unflagging support which their newspaper gave to the Jewish cause.

Whether in the *Colonial Times, Cornwall Chronicle, Launceston Examiner, Launceston Advertiser, Hobart Town Courier, Hobart Town Advertiser* or above all *Murray's Review*, the consistently friendly attitude of the Van Diemen's Land newspapers in the 1840s towards Jews as a group and their claims to equality was striking. The *Launceston Examiner*, 8 March 1843, described the improvement in the status of 'this once persecuted group' as one of the 'highest honors' of the 'present age'. The *Colonial Times*, 15 August 1843, reported thus the laying of the foundation stone of the Hobart synagogue:

> In accordance with that spirit of liberality and toleration which is one of the most significant and marked 'signs of the times', we rejoice at the admirable manner in which this interesting ceremony was conducted throughout, and at the gratification with which it was witnessed by the several denominations of Christians who were present. Sincerely do we join Mr. Nathan [the President] in the hope that they may long live to worship the God of their fathers in the temple of which the cornerstone is now laid.

Small wonder that Van Diemen's Land Jews, belonging to a group which in the age of emancipation had become obsessively

sensitive to manifestations of approval and disapproval from the
Gentile world around them, responded to the 'signs of the times'
in the manner of Benjamin Francis, President of the Launceston
Hebrew Congregation, who spoke on the occasion of the laying of
the foundation-stone of the Launceston synagogue, 26 September
1844:

> My Hebrew brethren and Christian friends . . . In the outpourings
> of my heart at this time, I thank God, we are assembled even in the
> earth's furthest limits . . . to cement by brotherly love the bonds
> which have beforetime bound the Hebrew community, alike amidst
> the fiercest political tyranny, and the bitterest religious persecution.
> The bright sun of modern intelligence, however, is fast dissipating
> the noisome vapours of intolerance and bigotry, and mankind now
> learn, that their social, moral and religious happiness depends not in
> religious dominancy, but rather in the exercise of love, benevolence,
> and good will from one to the other. The example my Christian
> friends have given this day of the absence of religious bigotry will
> be known in all lands, and shall be remembered when the pulsation
> of these generous hearts shall repose in the cold grave.[58]

Colonial opinion being on their side, the Jews' struggle for
equality in Van Diemen's Land came to depend on the outcome
of the twin movements for a cessation of transportation and for
responsible government. When in the early 1850s some measure of
responsible government was won, the Legislative Council decided
unanimously in October 1854 to grant state aid to the Jewish
religion. When Van Diemen's Land ceased to be the 'jail of the
Empire' and became Tasmania, it also ceased to be a Christian
state.

In the Jews' struggle in the various Australian colonies for equal
religious rights, Van Diemen's Land under Franklin and Eardley-
Wilmot thus had the distinction of representing the extreme case of
inequality. Nowhere else in the Australian colonies was the Christian-state view expounded as authoritatively and applied as consistently as in Van Diemen's Land: Jewish convicts were discriminated
against and free Jewish settlers were refused land for a cemetery.
And this refusal transcended the narrow limits of that island: in
conjunction with the New Zealand case it helped to shape the
policy of the Colonial Office regarding Jewish claims for a share
in state aid to religion.

From Christian to Liberal State:
Van Diemen's Land 1852-1855

When in 1844 the Jews of Launceston and Hobart learned from Sir Moses Montefiore that the Secretary of State had been 'unable to contravene the provisions of the colonial Act',[1] they must have realized that nothing short of the amendment of the Franklin Church Act could do away with their disability. Yet this was out of the question as long as the Legislative Council of Van Diemen's Land, composed of government members and nominees, remained unrepresentative and had virtually no legislative powers. Jews seem to have bided their time until early in 1852 when, in implementation of the Australian Colonies' Government Act, a partly elected Legislative Council, the 'Blended Council' was established.[2] They were meanwhile active, however, on another section of the front in renewing the fight for the religious rights of Jewish convicts. Not long after the death of the despotic Comptroller-General of Convicts, Captain Matthew Forster, in 1846, they approached his more enlightened and humane successor, Dr J. S. Hampton, on behalf of the Jewish convicts. They seem to have been able to gain some considerable concessions, for he promised to issue instructions that

> all Prisoners of the Jewish Persuasion not actually under a sentence would have leave to refrain from work and attend Synagogues in Hobart and Launceston on Sabbaths when present in these Towns and all pass-holders to refrain from labour at the Stations on Sabbaths.[3]

Dr Hampton seems to have kept his promise, at least for a time, for the Hobart Hebrew Congregation made arrangements that all Jewish convicts who attended the synagogue services on Sabbaths would be provided with two meals.[4] An enquiry was sent to the Chief Rabbi in London as to the religious status of Jewish convicts, asking whether they were eligible to help make up a religious quorum; he replied that convicts were eligible but that no religious honours should be conferred on them.[5] Thus for some time Jewish convicts in Van Diemen's Land enjoyed equal religious rights, and perhaps even privileges, for it may have been rather difficult to keep Jewish convicts, whose rest-day was Saturday, at work on Sundays.

Early in 1852 there was good reason to renew the struggle for a share in state aid to religion. The Australian Colonies Government Act of 1850-1 which under Schedule C had set aside the sum of £15,000 in aid to religion, did not as much as mention the word 'Christian', but referred to 'Public Worship'.[6] The new Legislative Council which met on New Year's Day 1852 was known to consist largely of 'liberals', all its sixteen elected members as distinct from the eight nominees having been returned on the anti-transportation platform.[7] Moreover the Lieutenant-Governor, William Denison, in his opening speech to the new Legislative Council, announced his intention to introduce a new, more comprehensive Church Bill which would provide state aid to 'every religious denomination'.[8]

Promptly the members of the Hobart Hebrew Congregation wrote to the Governor asking him to recommend that the Legislative Council 'make provision in the present estimates for the support of the ministers and for the erection and repair of the dwellings and places of the Jewish Church'. They reminded him of the promise of his opening speech and asked for an interview at which they could present a Petition.[9] In the Petition[10] they referred to the 'great grievance' that they were excluded from state aid derived from that general revenue to which they equally with others contributed. They complained that in the past they had 'been under the necessity' of erecting synagogues in Hobart and Launceston, and supporting their ministers, from their private resources. They urged that 'so long as the Government provides for other Churches from the general revenue your Petitioners are in justice and equity entitled to have a fair proportion of that revenue appropriated to the support of the Jewish Church', and demanded that they be placed 'upon a footing of equality with other Colonists in the administration as well of the ecclesiastical as of the secular concerns of the Government'. They invoked the precedent of the West Indian colonies where state aid was given to 'the Jewish Church in common with other Churches' and referred to the vote of the Legisla-

tive Council of Victoria of 30 December 1851 in favour of the
extension of state aid to the Melbourne Hebrew Congregation.

Nothing further was heard of this Petition. Denison may well
have assured the petitioners that his projected Church Bill would
take care of their claims. There can be little doubt that he intended
to make his Church Bill as comprehensive as possible. In his despatch about it to Earl Grey on 15 September 1851 he observed that
it would make provision 'for the maintenance of the clergy of all
religious persuasions without exception, placing all upon exactly
the same footing'.[11] At the time, Denison was self-consciously
proud that he belonged 'neither to High Church or Low Church,
Broad Church or Narrow Church' and convinced that his views
'when developed, will be found to be more truly liberal than those
of the most ultra opponents of Government'.[12] The Church Bill
which he introduced into the Legislative Council in July 1853 was
'truly liberal' in so far as it would have opened the door to Jewish
participation in state aid. The first clause of the Bill proposed to
repeal all previous Church Acts; these had specifically referred to
'certain ministers of the Christian religion'.[13] The new preamble
proposed instead to make 'general provision for the support and
advancement of Religious Worship in this colony', deliberately
leaving 'religion' undefined.[14] Moreover, clause 29 of the Bill defined the 'minister' eligible to receive state aid in the broadest possible terms as:

> any person who shall for the time being be the religious instructor
> or preceptor of any body of persons of any religious denomination,
> and who shall officiate in the performance of the worship of such
> religious denomination, according to the forms, rites, and ceremonies
> thereof, by what name, title, or designation soever such persons may
> by such body of persons of such religious denomination be styled...[15]

Small wonder that a Bill which studiously avoided the word
'Christian' was soon decried by some of its opponents as 'philo-
sophically indifferent' since it acknowledged neither 'Moses, Confucius, Mahomet nor Christ' and was accused of abolishing the
Christian religion 'so far as it can be done by laws'.[16] The Bill encountered strong opposition from diverse groups, Christian-state
men, staunch voluntaryists and a mixed bag of 'friends of civil and
religious liberty'. These organized public meetings[17] and presented
numerous petitions against the Bill.[18] Both liberal and conservative
opinion in the colony was dead set against the Bill, though for very
different reasons. Conservatives opposed it because in their opinion

it destroyed the 'Christian character' of the Van Diemen's Land community 'by admitting to equal rights the Christian and the infidel',[19] and foreshadowed the eventual abolition of state aid 'at no very distant period'.[20] Liberals fought it in spite of its 'perfect impartiality', because they feared it would increase the dependence of the churches on the state and would allow the state to interfere in the financial affairs of the various denominations.[21]

In the Legislative Council members as far apart as 'Churchman' W. S. Sharland, a devout Anglican, and T. D. Chapman—the leader of the anti-transportationists—who was a 'voluntaryist', moved for delay at the first reading of the Bill. In these circumstances the Bill, which would have enabled Jews to participate in state aid, was withdrawn by the Acting Colonial Secretary, W. T. N. Champ.[22] He did not insist on a second reading in view of the strong opposition, and in the belief that the British Parliament was about to legislate for the colonial churches in connection with the new constitution for the Australian colonies. The outcome must have been somewhat disappointing to Hobart Jews. Apparently a Bill, however broadminded and inclusive, which allowed the state to interfere in the internal affairs of religious congregations, could not command the support of colonial liberals. They seem to have veered more towards voluntaryist solutions and the eventual separation of church and state, and seem to have preferred the American answer to the problem of a multi-denominational society (no state aid to any religion) to the French solution (impartial endowment of all religions under state control).[23]

With the failure of Denison's Church Bill in 1853 the discriminatory Franklin Church Act remained in force and restricted state aid for 'Public Worship' to 'certain ministers of the Christian religion'.[24] Moreover, with the passing of the Clergy Pensions Bill in September 1854 which put state-aided clergymen on the same footing as public servants for pensions and cost of living adjustments,[25] it must have appeared to Hobart Jews that the existing Church Acts were there to stay and that their exclusion from state aid would continue indefinitely, unless they did something about it. In October 1854 they again petitioned the Legislative Council for state aid.[26]

As in their 1852 Petition, they complained of it as a 'heavy grievance' that they were taxed for state aid to religion while others received that aid; Schedule C referred to 'Public Worship' but they were excluded from its provisions. They quoted precedents from Jamaica and Canada and referred to the recent vote of the Legis-

lative Council in New South Wales in favour of the extension of
state aid to the Jewish congregation in Sydney. Aware of the constitutional difficulties in the way, they petitioned the Legislative
Council of Van Diemen's Land to 'take such measures as You may
deem best to obtain for the Jewish Church in this Colony a proportionate allowance from the Revenue for the support of Public
Worship'. Soon after, T. D. Chapman, the liberal member for
Hobart, presented a series of resolutions to the Legislative Council
'to place the Jew on the same footing as any other faithful subject
of Her Majesty who contributed to the public revenue.'[27] Chapman's resolutions paid tribute to the good citizenship of the Jews
of Van Diemen's Land and to their charity and public benefactions,
observing that this 'is to be more appreciated from the fact that
from their private funds they support their own poor, and pay the
whole expense of their own religious establishments.' Finally, they
affirmed the right of the 'Jewish Church' to a share in state aid:
'This House is of the opinion that the Jewish Church is, in proportion to the number of its members, justly entitled to a part of the
public Revenue of this Colony which is applied towards defraying
the expense of public Worship.'[28] The resolutions were adopted
unopposed[29] and incorporated into an Address to the Lieutenant-
Governor. Denison replied that he 'fully concurred' with the
opinion of the Council but could not give effect to its resolution
since it was not in his power to alter the amount reserved for Public
Worship.[30] Since both the Lieutenant-Governor and the Legislative
Council of Van Diemen's Land were 'unanimously of opinion' that
the 'Jewish Church' was 'justly entitled' to a share in state aid to
religion, T. D. Chapman on behalf of the Hobart Hebrew Congregation petitioned the Secretary of State, George Grey, to issue
instructions to that effect to the Lieutenant-Governor.[31]

In the despatch which accompanied Chapman's letter, Denison
showed himself earnestly in sympathy with the Jewish claims. He
suggested as a way out from all difficulties that a sum of £150
which had been declined by the Baptist minister be paid instead to
the Jewish rabbi as a temporary expedient, 'until some Legislative
enactment of a more comprehensive character than the present
Church Act can be passed, placing all Religious Communities
upon an equal footing.'[32] At the same time, prompted by Phineas
Moss in Hobart,[33] Sir Moses Montefiore in London sent to the
Secretary of State a resolution of the Board of Deputies of British
Jews in support of the claims of the Jews of Van Diemen's Land.[34]

This time there was no need for such lobbying and petitioning.

Lord John Russell was now Secretary of State. He informed the new Governor Sir Henry Young, that 'full power is given by the Imperial Act 13 & 14 Vic. Cap. 59 to the Governor and the colonial Legislature, subject to the Queen's pleasure, to alter the sum appropriated to Public Worship in Van Diemen's Land.'[35] When this message reached Hobart in September 1855, T. D. Chapman moved in the Legislative Council to address the Governor to place on 'Schedule C Part 3, of the Estimates of Expenditure for the year 1856 the sum of One hundred Pounds in aid of the salary of the minister of the Jewish Church in Hobart Town; and the sum of Fifty Pounds in aid of the salary of the minister of the Jewish Church in Launceston.'[36]

The debate on this motion[37] is of particular interest. As the only full-scale discussion of the question of Jewish religious equality in the Legislative Council of Van Diemen's Land, it affords some knowledge of the opinions and arguments of both the supporters and the opponents of the extension of state aid to the Jewish religion.

On one side were most of those who believed in religious equality, and most believers in the voluntary principle in religion and the eventual abolition of state aid. On the other side, against the grant to Jewish ministers, were believers in the Christian state, or very consistent abolitionists of state aid. These opponents of the grant insisted that 'there should be some limit somewhere' to state aid, as W. S. Sharland put it, and this limit, in their opinion, was reached when the four recognized Christian denominations, the Anglicans, Presbyterians, Catholics and Wesleyans, were supported. True, Captain William Langdon, as devout an Anglican as he was conservative, was prepared to go beyond that limit to vote money for 'the conversion of the Jews'. The only and rather feeble version of the Christian-state argument came from a Mr Knight who urged that 'the encouragement of the Christian religion was for the interest of the state' since it 'supported the state'. By 'Christianity' he understood the 'Presbyterians as well as the Established Church' who were 'within the pale of Christianity' and seems to have had reservations with regard to 'the Romish religion'. This definition of Christianity was not acceptable to H. F. Anstey, a liberal convert to Catholicism, who repaid Knight in kind: 'He was not aware that they were all Christians. They were a great number of infidels in all likelihood'.

A majority of those who spoke during the debate seem to have been in favour of the eventual abolition of all state aid to religion;

F

but they arrived at very different conclusions about the question under discussion. A. Douglas and the Solicitor-General, Francis Smith, claimed that as consistent abolitionists they could not make an exception in favour of the Jews. The Solicitor-General thought that 'the right principle was to get rid of all state support' for state aid was bound to be indiscriminate and absurd: 'If the shrine of Bacchus was to be set up he would be worshipped for he had a number of followers' and the 'Bacchantes' too might send a Petition to the Legislative Council as well as the Jews. On the other hand there was a majority of abolitionists among the supporters of the grant to Jews. These seem to have felt that this was the wrong occasion to begin implementing the voluntary principle. It was only a 'just and liberal principle' that 'while . . . state support to religion was maintained . . . the Jews were entitled as fully as any other denomination'. The Colonial Secretary, Champ, was even prepared to grant such aid to the Chinese. Dr William Crooke, the chief abolitionist spokesman and a leading supporter of the Jewish claim, urged the absurdity of state aid which paid the Jewish rabbi to 'instruct his people that Christianity was a lie' and the Christian clergymen to say the opposite. But the Jewish claim transcended the colonial controversy over state aid and was part of the general world-wide movement towards Jewish emancipation:

> it was their duty to second the liberal measure now in course of adoption all over the world with regard to the oppressed and perse-cuted portion of the human family—the Jews. Why should it be said that in Tasmania they were behind in that movement and that they should be less liberal in their feelings than the whole civilised world.

T. D. Chapman's motion was passed by 13 to 7 votes.[38]

If Dr Crooke had shown himself aware of the wider issue in-volved in the extension of state aid to the Jews of Hobart and Launceston, so were those Jews themselves. The importance which they attributed to their victory can be gauged from the letter which Phineas Moss wrote to Isaac Foligno, President of the Board of Deputies of British Jews. He thanked the Board for its assistance and reported that £150 had been placed on the Estimates for 1856: 'This amount however inconsiderable in a pecuniary view at first sight will be of importance ultimately, in proving the equal *status* of the Jews with the other subjects of Her Majesty in the colonies generally.'[39]

Thus with the vote of the Legislative Council in September 1855, Jews in Van Diemen's Land achieved equality with the

Christian denominations in the eyes of the state, and like them were
recipients of state aid until its abolition in 1869.[40] They even began
by getting the salary of the Baptist minister out of Schedule C,
and not a special grant. If they looked back to their dismal failure
of 1843 and their humiliation at the hands of a very Christian Governor, they had now after twelve years good reason to rejoice in
their achievement and to feel at ease in a society where both public
opinion and the legislature had shown sympathy for their aspiration to equality. The 'Resolutions' of the Legislative Council of
October 1854 read like a song of praise to their public spirit and
liberality. During the crucial debate of October 1855, even those
who, like Captain Langdon, spoke and voted against the extension
of state aid to the Jews, 'bore honourable testimony' to their good
citizenship.

Small wonder that Phineas Moss in his letter of thanks to T. D.
Chapman felt that 'a new enlightened era has dawned over us'.[41]
His confident optimism was shared by T. D. Gregson, the colony's
leading radical and democrat who in the debate on the Jewish
claim to state aid proclaimed his voluntaryist and liberal-democratic credo:

> He thought all religions were getting on very well without [state]
> interference—the Christian Church and the Jewish one. He was one
> who was willing to permit persons to follow their own religious
> course, and to get to heaven in their own way. He thought that in
> the middle of the 19th century men were becoming so liberal that if
> the bones of Tom Paine were raised and put together again, he
> would get followers.[42]

Jews in a Paradise of Dissent:
South Australia 1846-1851

The London philosophical radicals and financiers and the Protestant dissenters who were largely responsible for the foundation of the South Australian colony[1] were determined to have the principle of religious equality realized there.[2] From the very beginning it was stressed that this new colony would be wedded to the voluntary principle and would 'suit emigrants of every sect, as it will be under the charge of a Jew, a Roman Catholic, a Unitarian and a Church of England man'.[3]

The appointment of Jacob Montefiore, a wealthy Jewish banker of the City of London with Australian interests and connections, as one of the original Commissioners for the colony was generally regarded as a concession to liberal sentiment. Thomas Spring-Rice, Chancellor of the Exchequer, who seems to have been responsible for this appointment, was one of the early champions of Jewish emancipation in England.[4] Thus Moses Montefiore, the well known and greatly respected Jewish investment-banker and philanthropist, met no difficulty when lobbying Spring-Rice on behalf of his cousin Jacob. His diary records with satisfaction a visit he paid to Spring-Rice in May 1835 to thank him for having at 'his request' appointed Jacob Montefiore 'one of Her Majesty's Commissioners for the Colonisation of South Australia'.[5] At a time when in England Jews were still labouring under civil and political disabilities and were not yet admitted even to municipal offices, this appointment augured well for the position of Jews in the new colony.

In the colony, provision was made for the appointment of a colonial chaplain of the Church of England,[6] but there was no other breach of the voluntary principle for the first ten years. The small number of well-off Jewish merchants, importers, storekeepers, clothiers, innkeepers and landowners who had come mainly from London but also from Sydney and had settled in the colony before 1846[7] enjoyed full civil and political rights and a considerable social standing and prestige. After a three months' visit to the colony in 1843, Jacob Montefiore described it as a veritable paradise of dissent. Observing that the 'principles of civil and religious liberty are intermixed with the foundation of South Australia', he reported that the numerous religious denominations which he found in Adelaide enjoyed 'the opportunity to worship God according to the dictates of their consciences' and were 'secure from the domination of any religious sect'.[8] Listing a rich variety of sects, he made no mention of Jews. These were still very few—probably no more than ten—and were only just beginning to organize themselves into a religious group.[9]

As in other colonies, the first collective action was for a burial place. The need arose in August 1843 when Nathaniel Philip Levi, an early Jewish settler, died. His son Philip Levi, and Eliezer Montefiore as spokesman for the Jewish group, asked the Governor to allot a portion of the public cemetery for the needs of the members of the Jewish persuasion.[10] This request was immediately granted. E. L. Montefiore was invited to become a member of the Board of Trustees of the cemetery,[11] and Emanuel Solomon, a merchant and auctioneer, fenced the new allotment.

In 1844 there were a mere twenty-five Jews in the colony; fifteen lived in and near Adelaide, the rest in the country.[12] This small group which had a bare margin above the minimum number of a religious quorum (*Minyan*) of ten, began to assemble in the house of the merchant Burnett Nathan on the Jewish festivals. By 1846 the number had risen to fifty-eight (fifty-one in Adelaide and seven in the country).[13] In that year, for the first time, their full equality was questioned.

Lieutenant-Governor Robe introduced state aid to the Christian religion. As a High Churchman and 'Tory of Tories' he would have liked to assist only the Church of England, and would have introduced a 'system of public education in connexion with the Church of England under the guidance of its ministers'. But he was aware that this 'would be unwelcome to a large proportion of the colonists'[14] and realistic enough to take account of the influential and vociferous dissenters and of the traditions of religious equality which were firmly planted in the colony. Nor could he ignore the precedent of the Bourke Church Act of 1836 which had been implemented with the blessing of the Colonial Office in New South

Wales and in Van Diemen's Land. Both Robe's speech which broached the subject of state aid[15] at the opening session of the Legislative Council on 24 June 1846, and the nominee John Morphett's motion of 17 July which Robe inspired,[16] referred specifically to 'different sects of Christians'.

The small group of Jews in the colony acted promptly. While Robe's scheme was still under fire from the voluntaryists who wanted the state to 'let [religion] alone',[17] Major T. S. O'Halloran on behalf of the Jews of Adelaide presented a Petition in the Legislative Council on 4 August 1846.[18] The petitioners urged that they were 'entitled by law to all the privileges enjoyed by their fellow-colonists' and demanded their full share of 'any grant . . . for religious or educational purposes, out of the public revenues, to which they so largely contribute'. On 19 August Morphett's motion that the sum of £1,110 10s be introduced into the supplementary estimates for 1846 in aid of the 'different sects of professing Christians in proportion to their numbers', was passed.[19] Only two staunch voluntaryists, Captain C. H. Bagot and Samuel Davenport, voted against it. Major O'Halloran promptly moved, seconded by the Advocate-General W. Smillie, that £2 18s be inserted in the supplementary estimates for the support of the Jewish religion. He urged that the Jews in the colony had as much right as others to participate in the grant; they were 'highly respectable', contributed largely to the revenue and had 'all the privileges of British subjects'. Governor Robe tried to have O'Halloran's motion ruled out of order because the original motion had succeeded in restricting state aid to Christian sects. Morphett the mover waived this objection declaring that he would like to see the principle of O'Halloran's motion carried out. He even suggested 'a substantive motion' for a grant of £5 16s for the Jews. Robe objected that this would give the Jews 'twice as much as the Christians'. The Colonial Secretary, Alfred Mundy, a devout churchman and conservative, took the view that such a grant could not be 'of the slightest use' to the Jews and would look ridiculous in the estimates as a separate item. Neither objector questioned the principle of Jewish equality, and O'Halloran and the two voluntaryists, Bagot and Davenport, stressed that principle. A token grant, however small, would establish a precedent; although there were only fifty-eight Jews in the colony, many more might come. Captain Bagot had the satisfaction of reminding those who had voted in favour of state aid to religion that they had created the Jewish problem; if the grant to a non-

Christian religion was irksome to Robe, the trouble was of his own making.[20]

O'Halloran's motion was carried without opposition. Robe asked petulantly, 'and do you mean to propose Pagans?' In his effort to support Anglicans he was now not merely supporting obnoxious dissenters, but even Jews. Both Captain Bagot and Major O'Halloran made the most of Robe's question and answered 'yes' to it. Bagot as a voluntaryist was glad to reduce the whole principle of state aid to absurdity. O'Halloran was not yet a voluntaryist but seems to have relished the opportunity of demonstrating his liberalism and of needling the Governor into the bargain: 'Certainly, I have been in all parts of the world, and have seen much of the natives of India, and bear my testimony that more upright and honest men do not exist.'[21]

Voluntaryists lost no time in exploiting the extension of state aid to a non-Christian religion, in order to discredit state aid as such. The editor of the *South Australian Register*, John Stephens, enjoyed himself richly: 'The Governor's droll question "do you mean to propose Pagans?" is very amusing. Pagans! Of course! and everything and everybody else.' Conveniently forgetting that the issue involved in the vote to Jewish religion was that of religious equality, he taunted the Christian state-aiders who were now willy-nilly aiding the Jewish religion and above all the Rev. W. J. Woodcock, the only clergyman who had been imprudent enough to preach a sermon in favour of state aid:

> What our Jewish fellow-colonists will do with the money granted to them by their Christian rulers for the propagation of their creed, is matter for curious speculation. It is conjectured that they will give the tithe of the 58 shillings to the Rev. Woodcock in the form of a 'shoulder and breast' of mutton and build a wurley-synagogue with the remainder. Whether or not Mr. Woodcock will officiate at the opening, as temporary High-Priest, has not transpired.[22]

Similarly the spokesmen of the chief voluntaryist fighting body, 'The South Australian League for the Maintenance of Religious Freedom in the Province', rubbed in the point that 'the funds of the State are placed at the disposal of religious bodies professing themselves averse to Christianity'.[23]

For the Jews the vital question was neither state aid nor the voluntary principle, but equal rights. In 1848 *after* their equal religious rights had been officially recognized, the newly-founded Adelaide Hebrew Congregation adopted the 'voluntary principle' and resolved that 'no assistance be applied for from H. M. Colonial Government'.[24] We may assume that the Adelaide leaders who were also members of the Sydney Synagogue[25] were well informed of Governor Gipps's refusal to give state aid to the Jews of Sydney. By claiming an equal share while the first state aid measure was still under debate, they avoided a disappointment similar to that of their brethren in New South Wales. £2 18s in 1846 and £5 16s in 1847 were merely symbolic sums; but what they symbolized was a full and successful assertion of equal rights for the Jewish religion in South Australia. An important precedent had been established.

The liberal and tolerant climate of South Australia which had shown itself in this unanimous vote was further illustrated when Robe, who certainly was not in sympathy with this wide interpretation of his Act, felt the need to apologize for the difficulties he had made. Referring to the grant in aid of the Jewish religion on 1 September 1846, he declared:

> He was glad it so happened. His expressions during a former discussion had been misinterpreted. He was far from being disinclined to treatment of that body with every proper consideration. He had been much among them and it had been in his power to be of no considerable service to persons of the Jewish nation by protecting them from the persecutions of Mahometans . . . The proportionate grant was necessarily small, but in another year it might be more considerable.[26]

Reporting to Earl Grey on the introduction of state aid to religion, Robe mentioned that upon the motion of a private member a similar grant was extended to the Jews 'merely upon principle' the amount being 'too trifling to be of any practicable utility'.[27] The attitude of the Colonial Office to this innovation, coming just after Governor FitzRoy of New South Wales had been censured for a similar grant, seems to have been one of regretful acquiescence. An unsigned minute to Robe's despatch to Benjamin Hawes, the Parliamentary Under-Secretary, drew attention to the fact that in contrast with FitzRoy's special grant in Sydney, to which 'Lord Grey had objected', the South Australian grant was 'part of a general measure'. If the colonists had decided to adopt such a general measure, 'Lord Grey would not oppose their wish, though he should regret it'.[28]

In Adelaide the Jews were very loosely organized and had not yet formed a congregation. They mainly met on the High Holydays and on similar occasions in a private residence. They had no minister and no actual use for these token grants of state aid; so they never collected the money.[29] This could not affect the principle of equality which the grants established, but it did assume some importance in connection with Governor Robe's more comprehensive Church Bill of 1847. This, which in its final form was to become Ordinance no. 10, was modelled on the Bourke Church Act of 1836. It replaced the indiscriminate *per capita* system of the 1846 State Aid Bill with one of state subsidy in proportion to the voluntary subscriptions of congregations who applied for it.[30] In its original form, its title and preamble were borrowed from the New South Wales model. The title made no reference to the Christian religion. It read: 'A Bill to promote the Building of Churches and Places of Worship and to provide for the Maintenance of Ministers of Religion.'[31] However on 21 July 1847 when the second reading of the Church Bill was passed and the Legislative Council went into committee, the Quaker Jacob Hagen moved to insert the word 'Christian' into the title before the word 'Worship': 'it was his intention . . . that the money should only be applied for the promotion of such religions as were entitled to the designation of Christian'.[32] Robe seconded Hagen's amendment. Major O'Halloran 'most decidedly' objected to it. Not only 'the Jewish persuasion would be excluded'; he held that 'if the Chinese, Hindoos or New Zealanders came to South Australia, he considered they would be as fully entitled to their quota as the members of any Christian Religion, upon the principle that they were equally contributing to the State.'[33] As in 1846 Robe was careful not to question the principle of religious equality. There could be other Bills for other religions. He understood that 'the Council was legislating for the Christian religion. The Bill for the promotion of Mohammedanism was not yet before them'.[34]

The amendment was carried and the word 'Christian' was inserted into the title of the new Church Bill; it passed its second reading on Robe's casting vote.[35] But its operation was limited to a trial period of three years ending in March 1850; Robe knew the strength of voluntaryist opposition to it, and he cannot have wished to strengthen the opposition by giving it broad grounds of religious liberty and equality. At the third reading of the Church Bill on 3 August 1847 Major O'Halloran took him at his word and asked him to 'introduce a Bill to give the Jews the same privileges as the Christians'.[36] The Registrar-General, Charles Sturt, asked whether O'Halloran spoke for the Jews or merely 'of his own opinion'. He did not want to legislate if the Jews would again fail to 'avail them-

selves of the measure'. Robe agreed, especially because the Jews
had not collected their grant of 1846: 'Until it was shown that it
was desired by the Jews, he would be sorry to lay such a measure
on the table'.[37] But neither Robe nor Sturt questioned the right of
Jews to a share in state aid to religion if they really wanted it.

Within a week there were twenty-four signatures—probably the
whole number of adult male Jews in Adelaide—on a Petition to the
Lieutenant-Governor and the Legislative Council. At the head of
the list were the names of J. B. Montefiore (he arrived in Adelaide
from London in 1846 and set up in business with his nephew and
future son-in-law E. L. Montefiore as importers and shipping
agents), Eliezer Levi Montefiore, Burnett Nathan and J. M.
Solomon. The Petition, presented by Major O'Halloran on 17
August 1847[38] asked that the Jews 'be placed upon the same footing
in proportion to their number as their Christian brethren', reminded
Robe and the Council of the precedent which had been established
in 1846, and appealed to them to 'carry out the same enlightened
principle'. As to their failure to collect the grant of the previous
year, 'their only motive for not having received it was the difficulty
in appropriating so small a sum'. They would claim it in future
'when they can devote it for the purpose for which it was intended'.[39]

Robe in reply promised to introduce a Bill into the Legislative
Council 'conferring upon the Jewish faith the same privileges respecting religion and education enjoyed by Christians'.[40] That he
intended to keep his promise is borne out by the correspondence
between the Colonial Secretary, Mundy, and E. L. Montefiore, the
main Jewish spokesman, regarding the mode of appointment of
trustees of a denomination which had no 'place of worship and
consequently no Minister or Congregation'.[41] On 25 August 1847
Mundy wrote:

> as His Excellency intends in pursuance of notice given in Council, to
> confer on the Jewish Community in this Colony similar privileges to
> those which have been recently accorded to other religious denomi-
> nations, His Excellency would feel obliged by your pointing out in
> what particular manner the Church Ordinance No. 10 would require
> to be modified in its application to the Body which you represent.[42]

The matter went no further, but that was almost certainly because the Jews, rather than the Lieutenant-Governor, let it drop.
Scarcely organized, without a place of worship and without a
minister, they were probably content that their religious equality

had in principle been accepted both by Robe and by the Council. There may have been stronger reasons, in positive support for voluntaryism. With their equality officially and repeatedly acknowledged, they could safely refuse the aid which some of the Christian sects were also refusing, as a matter of voluntaryist principle. Thus in the following year when a Jewish congregation was officially established and a subscription towards the building of a synagogue was opened, the congregational committee resolved unanimously that the subscription be raised 'upon the voluntary principle only, and that no assistance be applied for from H.M. Colonial Government' towards the furtherance of this object.' Instead they decided to appeal to the Jews of Sydney, Port Phillip, Hobart and Launceston and to their Christian fellow-citizens for financial support.[43] The staunchly voluntaryist *South Australian Register* now noted with considerable satisfaction that Adelaide Jews intended not to apply for 'any portion of the Government grant' and 'heartily recommended' 'those who can do so conscientiously to give their mites towards the good work, the more especially as many Hebrews have pecuniarily helped to rear some of our Christian places of worship.'[44] Likewise, when in 1850 the Jewish congregation was in debt and two of its leading members, J. M. Solomon and Morris Marks, proposed that assistance be sought from the state, a general meeting of the congregation defeated the proposal by 16 to 3 votes.[45]

Jewish support for the voluntary principle was made even plainer in 1851 when the final battle against state aid was waged in the colony. In 1850 the three years' trial period of the Church Ordinance expired, and a Legislative Council of eight nominees and sixteen elected members was about to be set up under the new constitution.[46] In the elections to the new Legislative Council in July 1851 state aid to religion was the main issue, and at least eleven of the elected members were committed to its abolition.[47] On 29 August, within a week of the Council's first meeting, E. C. Gwynne, a non-official nominee and a good Churchman, moved for the indefinite continuation of Ordinance no. 10.[48] Its title indicated its purpose, to provide for 'Churches and Chapels for Christian Worship' and for 'Ministers of the Christian Religion'.[49] A special general meeting of Adelaide Jews decided to petition the Legislative Council 'relative to a Measure now before them of the greatest importance to the Jews of this province.'[50] They asked E. L. Elder, a dissenter and a staunch voluntaryist, to present their 'Memorial' against Gwynne's Bill at its first reading. The Memorial expressed the Jewish point of view admirably:

> Your Memorialists observe with regret that a measure is about to be introduced into your Honourable Council for the purpose of granting aid in support of Christian religious worship.
>
> Your Memorialists have no wish whatever to receive aid from the revenue of the province for the support of their faith, but at the same time beg to call the attention of the Council to the fact of their contributing in an equal degree with the members of every faith to the support of the general revenue of the province.
>
> Your Memorialists therefore trust that your Honourable Council will not under any circumstances, permit class legislation, or any Bill to pass having as its object the exclusion of the Jews, or any other sect, from a participation in any portion of the revenue to which they are, as contributors thereto justly entitled.
>
> Your Memorialists feel convinced that your Honourable Council is composed of such men as will never permit an intolerant measure, such as that about to be introduced, to pass your Honourable Council, as it will no doubt appear to you, as it does to us, inequitable to compel us to support any other faith, who are not in like manner compelled to support us.
>
> Your Memorialists therefore feel that they may with full security trust your Council, either to throw out the Bill for granting aid to all Christian denominations, or that the terms of that Bill will be so altered as to admit all classes of religionists to claim the aid who may be disposed to receive it.[51]

As appears from their Memorial, the 'Members of the Jewish Faith, resident in South Australia' had come out in favour of the voluntary principle in religion while at the same time staking a claim to an equal share in state aid—or an equal right to refuse any aid that might be offered.

Gwynne's Bill was thrown out at its first reading by 13 votes to 10,[52] and state aid to religion was thus abolished in South Australia for good. This disposed of the question of Jewish religious equality.

The same liberal principle was applied to the General Education Act later in the year, when clause no. 2 of the proposed Education Bill was so framed as to make its provisions 'extend to the members of the Hebrew persuasion'[53] and was communicated to both the Catholic and Jewish congregations for their approval. It stipulated that

> in schools established or to be established under the provision of this Act, the aim shall be to introduce and maintain good secular instruction, based on the Holy Scriptures, apart from all theological and

controversial differences on discipline and doctrine; and that no denominational catechism be used.[54]

With Scripture readings pushed into the last half-hour of the school day and children of conscientious objectors allowed to leave school before the reading began, the Education Bill was certainly acceptable to Adelaide Jews. Indeed, J. B. Montefiore on behalf of the Jewish congregation welcomed it wholeheartedly in his communication to the Colonial Secretary:

> shall it pass as law I am satisfied, it will be a matter of no small rejoicing to the Community generally to find that the Legislature does not interfere in matters of religion which are to be left (as they ought to be) between Man and his Maker. It appears to me that the proposed clause will carry out every object that can be required by Dissenters of any denomination.[55]

Thus, by comparison with other parts of the world as well as other Australian colonies, South Australia surely deserved to be called 'Paradise of Dissent'. For Jews in Australia it was the best case, as Van Diemen's Land was the worst. Politically, South Australia offered its Jews equal rights and opportunities from the very beginning. Jacob Montefiore was one of its Commissioners. His brother, J. B. Montefiore, represented the 'Government of the Province of South Australia' in New South Wales. In 1855 John Lazar became Mayor of Adelaide[56] and in 1857 Morris Marks was a member of the Legislature,[57] *before* Jews were admitted in England to the House of Commons. At no stage was there the least attempt to question the bona fide citizenship of the Jewish settlers. Their religious rights were positively and officially affirmed in 1846 and 1847. Whatever objections were raised were feeble and rather apologetic, and did not challenge the principle of religious equality. Even the Colonial Office, reluctantly, had to acquiesce in the egalitarian policy of the legislature and the governor of South Australia.

But as the Gwynne Bill of 1851 showed, it was the abolition of state aid to religion and the introduction of a system of undenominational education, i.e. the final separation of church and state, which made Jewish religious equality really secure.

The Struggle in Victoria 1850-1855

Jews who settled in Port Phillip from 1839 onwards came from the neighbouring colonies—mainly from Sydney and Hobart or direct from London.[1] Like most settlers of Port Phillip and Melbourne they 'came free', untainted by convictism. They belonged to that group of young middle-class British-born Jews, many with small and some with larger means, who were attracted to Australia in the 1830s and 1840s by its commercial opportunities and promptly founded and manned the Jewish congregational institutions of Sydney, of Goulburn's 'little Jerusalem', Adelaide, Hobart, Launceston and Melbourne.

Early arrivals, the merchant Solomon Benjamin (who came in 1839 and was later joined by his brother and partner David) and the young and dynamic wholesale trader Michael Cashmore (he arrived in 1840) immediately established a Jewish Philanthropic Society. When in 1841 Asher Hyman Hart joined his brothers, the clothiers Edward and Isaac Hart, and set up in business as a draper and later as an auctioneer, he transformed what was then a mere philanthropic society and a small Jewish population of some fifty souls, into a proper Jewish Congregational Society, later and appropriately renamed 'Holy Congregation of the Remnant of Israel'.[2] In need of a properly consecrated cemetery, they applied for a grant of land and received one in May 1843.[3] Governor Gipps's grant and behaviour earned him the applause of the *Port Phillip Herald* of 27 April 1843 where it was contrasted with that of Sir John Franklin who 'most inhumanly refused'.[4] When in September 1843 the Melbourne Jewish leaders were about to apply for a grant of land for a synagogue they seem to have had second thoughts and bided their time until the Franklin affair in Van Diemen's Land had blown over.[5] They finally applied in February

1844 and received a valuable allotment for a synagogue at the top of Bourke Street.[6] The deed itself, coming as it did so soon after Franklin's refusal to make a similar grant to the Jews of Launceston, is an interesting document in so far as it explicitly accepted the Jewish religion as one which the state was concerned to promote:

> Know ye that in order to promote Religion and Education in our Territory of New South Wales We of our special Grace have granted . . . unto Asher Hyman Hart Michael Cashmore and Solomon Benjamin . . . all that piece or parcel of land . . . (Advertised as No. 5 in the Government Notice dated 11 October 1844) for the erection thereon of a Synagogue for the use of the Members of the Jewish Persuasion and for no other purpose whatsoever . . .[7]

When the small synagogue building was nearing completion in February 1848, it proved beyond the financial means of the Melbourne Hebrew Congregation. There were some twenty-five privileged members and ten mere seat-holders, representing a Jewish population of less than two hundred. Except for four well-off merchants, the members made modest livings as drapers, clothiers, outfitters and general dealers.[8] To pay its most urgent debts, the congregation borrowed £200 from the Melbourne Savings Bank, and let part of the synagogue ground.[9]

Asher Hyman Hart, the congregation's founder and stalwart president, may have been thinking for some time of getting some state aid. His opportunity came when Henry Moore (one of the six representatives of the Port Phillip district in the Legislative Council of New South Wales) was about to introduce a Bill in aid of the Churches of Port Phillip. Hart wrote to Moore in July 1850 to ask him to support a Jewish Petition for state aid—'although Melbourne Jews have to the present time refrained from asking the most trifling assistance from any but those of our own faith' they were now so impecunious they had no choice but apply for aid 'like other denominations'. True to the spirit of the victorious Port Phillip separation movement, and perhaps playing on Moore's notorious Port Phillip 'ultra-patriotism',[10] Hart added: 'what I now ask is but a trifle of Port Phillip money for a public service to be expended in Port Phillip.'[11]

On 30 July C. H. Ebden, a member for Port Phillip, presented a Petition on behalf of the Melbourne Jewish congregation to the Legislative Council of New South Wales. It said that the Jewish congregation could not pay its debts or its current expenses, and asked for a grant of £500 towards the completion of the synagogue-building and the liquidation of its debts.[12] On 9 August, after a short debate, the Council unanimously decided to address the Governor 'to cause to be placed on the Supplementary Estimates for the present year a sum not exceeding £500, for the purpose of enabling the members of the Jewish persuasion to complete their Synagogue and Minister's dwelling.'[13] As was to be expected, Governor FitzRoy had no choice but to refuse. In his reply of 13 August, he explained that in view of Earl Grey's despatch of 13 April 1847 he could not 'consider himself at liberty to comply with the present application, without previously obtaining the sanction of Her Majesty's Government.'[14]

So a new Petition went to Grey. Signed by 133 'Members of the Hebrew Faith', it referred 'with sorrow and disappointment' to the Governor's refusal to grant them the 'small sum' of £500 and asked the Secretary of State to direct the Governor to accede to 'the unanimous opinion of the entire Colony as expressed by their Representatives (all members of the various Christian denominations) in the Legislative Council.'[15]

The Petition reached London early in April 1851. The Colonial Office minutes suggest a softening or slight change of attitude towards Jewish claims to state aid. James Stephen was no longer there to oppose it strongly, as in 1847, on the ground of principle. Neither Gordon Gairdner nor Herman Merivale, Stephen's successor as Permanent Under-Secretary, expressed any views on the matter. Gairdner merely drew attention to Grey's despatch of 1847 and his censure of FitzRoy's grant to the Sydney congregation.[16] Benjamin Hawes, the Parliamentary Under-Secretary, reiterated his dissenting opinion: 'I know not why the Jews should be excluded from the benefit of a grant which is conceded to other religious bodies'.[17] This put Grey on the defensive. He now justified his refusal solely on procedural grounds. He conceded that 'there is no objection to Jews having the same assistance as other religious bodies (at least no objection on which it is necessary to insist)' but objected to grants being 'made by votes on the Estimates'.[18] They shall be made in the 'same manner and according to the same fixed rule' as applied to Christian denominations.[19] This might suggest some general softening of opposition, but it was still no immediate help to the Melbourne Jews, and it gave FitzRoy little reason to think that Grey had really ceased to 'certainly regret' the granting of state aid to Jews.[20] It did however suggest the next step. Melbourne Jews petitioned the new Legislative Council of

Victoria in December 1851 for a 'proportionate allowance' from the 'Public Revenue'. This, they claimed, was their 'just right' and in accordance with the 'liberal views of the age'. The Petition may have been deliberately vague when referring to 'Public Revenue', leaving ways and means to the Council.[21]

William Westgarth, the first member for Melbourne and the colony's outstanding and respected liberal and democrat, was asked to present the Jewish Petition. Seconded by the O'Connellite John O'Shanassy, the second member for Melbourne and acknowledged leader of its Irish-Catholic community, he moved on 30 December 1851 that 'The Persuasion of the Jews of this city be allowed to participate according to their numbers in the reservation for religious purposes, under the head of Schedule B.'[22] The debate[23] shows the liberal supporters of the Jewish claim outspoken and confident, and its conservative opponents unsure of themselves—they merely asked for delay on grounds of procedure, and were anxious not to challenge the 1847 instructions and the New South Wales precedent of 1849. Only the staunch Anglican R. W. Pohlman invoked the principle of the Christian state—'he had always considered that Christianity was the law of the land'. There was a very liberal tone in the first session of the Victorian legislature. Members vied with each other in praising the respectability and civic worth of the Melbourne Jewish community.

Westgarth, O'Shanassy and the radicals J. P. Fawkner and Henry Miller put the local claim to state aid into the wider perspective of mid-nineteenth-century liberalism and Jewish emancipation. Westgarth reminded them of the 'dark ages' when it would have been good enough to allow Jews to receive their lives and little else, 'but times were now changed'. J. P. Fawkner (like Lowe, Robert Grant, Wentworth and Disraeli before him), as if to disarm the Christian-state men, harped on the Jewish ancestry of Christianity: 'The great founder of our religion was himself a Jew. David was a Jew. The Apostles, the promulgators of our faith, were Jews and had given to us a code of laws, which but for them we should never have had.' Christians were therefore under 'great obligations' to the Jews and were bound to extend to them 'fair play'. Fawkner thought that generally 'great changes' had taken place in Britain with regard to the Jews, and they had 'found a place in the Commons' House'.[24] He called upon members to 'spare no exertions in order that Victoria might be the first of the British colonies to extend to the Jews their full rights as British citizens.'

The timid objections of the Colonial Secretary, William Lons-

G

dale, who referred to Grey's despatch to prove that the object of Westgarth's motion could only be achieved by an amendment of the Church Act, drew an angry and defiant outburst from J. S. Johnston, an editor of the liberal *Argus* and a radical democrat. He appealed to the House not to do an 'act of injustice' merely because 'they were told so' by a despatch from Grey which 'went the length of saying that he regretted that the Jewish religion was to be supported in the colonies'. O'Shanassy was 'surprised' at the opinion Grey had expressed for

> he must have been aware that reserve grants of land had already been made to the Jews and consequently there could be no doubt as to the principle. The Crown itself had recognised the claims of the Jew by the very circumstance of making him a grant of land for religious purposes.

It seems to have been generally agreed at the end of the debate that the proper procedure was to bring in a Bill to amend the Church Act to include the Jewish religion. This was the course suggested by the Auditor-General (C. H. Ebden). Westgarth then withdrew his motion and summed up the liberal climate of the debate when he observed: 'it must be highly gratifying to the members of the Jewish persuasion to hear the unanimous and favourable expression of the House regarding them.'

On 16 September 1852 Westgarth brought the question of state aid to Jews once again to the notice of the Legislative Council. Yet contrary to what might have been expected in the light of the 1851 debate, he failed to make a frontal attack on the difficulties arising from the preamble of the Church Act and from Grey's despatch. He tried to evade the constitutional problem by having recourse to another variant of the vaguely worded Jewish Petition of 1851. He moved that the Legislative Council request the Governor to 'place upon the Estimates of the ensuing year a sum of money in aid of the Community of the Jews in this colony proportionately to similar aids presently awarded to other religious denominations of the Colony.'[25] This would avoid amending the Church Act, while 'proportionately to similar aids' should ward off objections to special treatment. As we shall see, Westgarth thus enabled the opponents of state aid to Jews to take advantage of the legal difficulties which his motion had shirked and to force an issue when its weakness had become evident.

It was a poor line of action but it occasioned a good debate. Westgarth led: 'The question was one entirely of principle and not of facts and statistics and on principle he founded a claim for the Jews to partake and possess all privileges which were enjoyed by other denominations.' He himself was in favour of the abolition of state aid to religion, but as long as it was continued all were entitled to it. He believed there were some thousand Jews in the colony,[26] and many of that class were not only of the 'first respectability' but were numbered among 'their own intimate friends and acquaintances'. He was not aware that there were any obstacles to Jews becoming members of the colonial legislature; he knew that in Jamaica Jews were members of the House of Assembly and received state aid for their religious institutions. In the same vein, O'Shanassy, consistent with his desire to accord to all classes 'exact and equal rights', looked at the Jewish claim not as a religious but as a political question: 'the Jews look to equality in receiving the grant, in the light of a question of liberty and nothing more'. Similarly, Johnston drew attention to the 'very smallness' of the share in state aid to which the Jews were entitled—a mere £32—as proof that it was only asked for as 'a matter of right and principle'.[27]

For once, the opponents of Jewish religious equality felt sufficiently confident to meet its advocates on their own ground of principle. R. W. Pohlman (Chairman of Quarter Sessions) agreed that the question should be looked at as 'one of principle' and urged that 'the law of the land initiated the principle that such grants were to be confined to Christian sects'. As to the argument of the Jewish ancestry of Christianity, he referred to the debate 'at home' and the view put forward there that 'Christianity was Judaism perfected and . . . Judaism Christianity commenced' and urged that until 'Judaism became Christianity' the principle of the Church Act should not be departed from. He trusted that therefore the House, 'however reluctantly', would fulfil their duty 'as members of a Christian legislature'. In a similar vein the Attorney-General W. F. Stawell, a devout Anglican and an Anglo-Irish gentleman, urged that 'the State as a Christian State was bound to support Christianity'. Another archetypal representative of the Anglo-Irish Protestant gentry which dominated the government and the first Legislative Council of Victoria was Thomas T. à Beckett.[28] He went to the length of turning the problem inside out:

> It would be regarded by the Jews as a slur, for that people considered that to receive such aid from Gentiles would be as it were a profanation . . . The Jews stood alone in their religion and mixed not with any other class. They were a peculiar people and would be likely to refuse such aid . . .[29]

O'Shanassy observed that he 'thought it exceedingly strange that all those persons who lived in the city and were well acquainted with the wishes of the Jews should be exactly of the opposite way of thinking of Mr. à Beckett'. Apart from betraying 'old world' prejudice, à Beckett and William Rutledge, a conservative pastoralist (squatter), were out to discredit Westgarth's motion on the ground that he and his seconder Henry Miller did not really want state aid for the Jews, but as abolitionists aimed 'to do away with the grant altogether and so had brought forward this motion'.

à Beckett had imported into the debate some English arguments against Jewish emancipation. Henry Miller countered with another import, an argument with an unmistakable Macaulayan touch:

> It was an argument against the Jews that they did not identify them-selves with the country in which they lived and as they were conse-quently not such good subjects they were not entitled to the same privileges as their fellow-subjects. But now when the Jews came forward both here and at home, and asked to identify themselves with the country by taking offices and by asking this aid, now was the time to wipe away this single last argument . . .

Jews, he urged, asked for the grant not as a 'pecuniary benefit' but 'solely as a matter of principle' and as being 'a full recognition of their rights as Jewish citizens'. He appealed obliquely to the self-esteem of his fellow-legislators when he concluded: 'as men be-come enlightened . . . the Jew had increased in estimation and his position was now always in proportion to the degree of civilisation which the country he lived in had arrived at.'

In the course of this debate it became increasingly clear that, apart from those who were opposed to a grant on principle, there were others who doubted whether Westgarth's motion was com-petent to overcome the legal difficulties. The Colonial Secretary, the Attorney-General and the Auditor-General had made it clear that the Governor was bound to refuse. Dr Francis Murphy, a moderate conservative, would vote the Jews 'any sum they might require', even though he could not agree that all sects were entitled to state aid, for 'there were such men as Mormons and Socialists and such as resided in abodes of love'. He was, however, sure the Governor could not assent even if the motion were passed and he recommended therefore that Westgarth withdraw the motion in its present form. Westgarth tried to do so; but this was objected to. His motion was then defeated by 11 votes to 10.[30] With the excep-tion of Dr Murphy and Rutledge, all the Noes were government members and nominees.[31] Only one nominee member, Colonel J. Anderson, known for his courage and humane firmness as commander of Norfolk Island, voted in favour of the motion.

Melbourne Jews had good reason to feel alarmed by both the tenor of the 1852 debate and the adverse vote. If in 1850 and 1851 they had chiefly wanted some money, the 1852 debate must have warned them that nothing less than their equality in the colony of Victoria was the subject under debate. This debate could equally well have been held in the British House of Commons, if not on state aid to Jews, then with regard to their political emancipation.

There was worse to come.

The gold rush brought social crisis, and some fear for law and order. The liberal tone of the legislature took a sharp conservative turn. On 30 November 1852 the voluntaryists moved to have state aid to religion abolished altogether. Besides the general voluntaryist principle, the movers made it clear that they had also in mind the 'civil rights' of the Jews to whom 'assistance was not awarded by the Government'.[32]

This Johnston Abolition Bill (Public Worship Schedule B Alteration Bill) was roundly beaten by 15 votes to 8.[33] Its defeat reflected a widespread feeling that in the social crisis through which the colony was passing, religion, believed to be the 'cheapest police', ought to receive more assistance from the state rather than none.[34] Conservative advocates of state aid like Rutledge were encouraged to take the initiative and to counter-attack. In January 1853 the Public Worship Promotion Bill was passed, increasing state aid to religion from £6,000 to £30,000 annually. Moreover, the Public Worship Promotion Bill, while repealing the Bourke Church Act, retained its Christian definition and thus perpetuated the exclusion of the Jewish religion from state aid.[35] The new preamble read: 'Whereas for the advancement of the Christian religion and the promotion of good morals in the colony of Victoria it is expedient to encourage the observance of Public Worship'. This did away with the old question whether 'Public Worship' in the Constitution Act of 1842 was to be interpreted in the light of the Bourke Church Act or not; as far as Victoria was concerned nothing was now public worship unless it was Christian. Not the Bourke Church Act or Grey's despatch of 1847, but a brand new Act passed by the Legislative Council of Victoria of its own free will, now denied the religious equality of Jews. Inequality was no longer a relic; it had become a new and active policy.

The worst was still to come. It was still possible to regard the setbacks of 1850, 1851 and 1852, and even the discriminatory preamble to the Public Worship Promotion Bill of 1853, as temporary. Jews and their allies could still pin their hopes to a new, more representative constitution and to the growth of liberalism in the colony. These hopes were shattered by the Public Worship clause of the new constitution.

The Select Committee which prepared the draft of the Constitution on the motion of O'Shanassy formulated the preamble of the Public Worship clause no. 68, later no. 60, to read: 'That for the advancement of religion and the promotion of good morals in the Colony of Victoria, the sum of £50,000 should be reserved on the Schedule for Public Worship, to promote the erection of buildings and the maintenance of Ministers of religion therein'.[36] This clause would have enabled any religion, unless morally objectionable, to receive state aid. For that very reason, conservatives saw it as a threat to the Christian state and worked hard to amend it. On 21 October 1853 the Attorney-General, W. F. Stawell, moved in the Select Committee that the word 'Christian' be inserted in the clause. He was beaten 4 to 2.[37] Undaunted, Stawell's cousin J. F. L. Foster, Colonial Secretary, grandson of an Anglican Bishop and son of a Tory M.P., moved on 16 February 1854 in the Legislative Council that the word 'Christian' be inserted before the word 'religion'. He also proposed to omit the words 'and the promotion of good morals', perhaps to drive home the point that religion undefined could include an immoral religion.[38]

J. P. Fawkner promptly counter-moved in favour of the words 'Hebrew and Christian Religions'. The debate centred on the question how Christianity and morality were to be defined and where the line should be drawn.[39] The liberal-sceptical point of view was put forward by O'Shanassy, the Collector of Customs (H. Childers), the Solicitor-General (R. Molesworth), Mark Nicholson and others who emphasized that the state was ill equipped to define what Christianity was, whereas its 'tribunals'—the police courts—decided every day what was morality and what was not. Therefore all sects, unless they were subversive of morals, were equally entitled to state aid. O'Shanassy urged 'their aim should be to establish religious equality as far as it was possible without injury to the maintenance of the social compact' while the Solicitor-General, in a liberal-sceptical vein, did not believe that

> every Christian sect promoted good morals. He would not be responsible for any of them. He would support Jews, Mahomedans, and

Pagans (Hear, Hear). He must either make himself responsible for the opinions of those he did support, or support them all.

On the other side, Foster warned of bogey-men. Hindus and Chinese were immigrating into the colony:

> The tenets of these often inculcated the commission of crime and immorality—as in the case of murder by the Thugs, or Polygamy by the followers of Confucius. The doctrines of these people were subversive of all morality according to Christian ideas and yet they might claim their share in the fund unless the amendment was adopted.

As to the question who was a 'Christian', Foster saw no difficulty there. He believed it could be 'determined' without consulting an encyclopaedia or even the Executive Council. He would adopt a confession of belief in Christianity as the test.

The wide range of reasons for supporting a Christian definition of the Public Worship clause is perhaps exemplified on the one hand by the diehard R. W. Pohlman, 'Episcopalian to the bone and the spinal marrow', who would exclude not only Jews but also Unitarians and on the other by W. Campbell, an ultra-conservative but more tolerant and accommodating in religious matters, who 'respected the Jews and did not object to give them aid by gratuity', but would not 'provide for them in a Constitution'.

Foster's amendment was carried by 19 to 13 votes.

In the short debate on Fawkner's amendment that the words 'and Hebrew' be added to the word 'Christian', Fawkner dwelt on the Jews' gift of the Bible to Christianity; he therefore 'desired to advance the Christian religion and to support the Jewish'. The Colonial Secretary did not appreciate Fawkner's finely drawn distinction:

> He testified to the good conduct and to the liberality and moral character of the Jews, but he thought it would read oddly in a statute-book to vote a grant in aid of Christianity and to admit the Jews to partake in it . . . There was a broad line of demarcation between Christianity and Judaism, which they could not easily get over, unless some ingenious person would prove that a Jew was another form of Christian.

The 'broad line of demarcation' was distinctly drawn when the vote was taken and Fawkner's amendment was lost by 15 to 16 votes.[40]

Thus the advocates of the Christian state succeeded in imposing a Christian definition on the Public Worship clause. The exclusion of the Jewish religion from the benefits of state aid was now about to be written not merely into the law but into the constitution of Victoria.

However quietly the Jewish community had received its setbacks in 1852 and 1853, in 1854 no one could have been left in doubt of its attitude to the proposed Public Worship clause. Immediately upon the vote of 16 February 1854 'against them and their co-religionists' a protest meeting was called for 22 February in the Melbourne synagogue. The general tenor of that meeting was fore-shadowed in a letter which appeared in the *Argus* on 21 February under the title 'Religious Persecution Has Not Yet Ceased in the Land.' 'Judaicus' put the Jewish grievance thus:

> To me and many of my co-religionists the matter seems inexplicable and even strange that in a new, rising and vigorous colony, feelings of prejudice and religious inequality should still exist and that creed should exercise an influence in determining the extent of privileges to be granted. It seems surprising that in a country free and en-lightened and whose legislators have introduced and carried measures extremely liberal, grand and comprehensive, there should yet exist the slightest feeling of religious prejudice . . . that the members of one faith should be set aside from receiving certain political privileges solely because some of their religious principles are not entirely in accordance with the other race . . .

In the hostility of *some* Legislative Councillors 'Judaicus' detected not 'reason and conviction' but a 'slight inherent feeling of pre-judice' which intruded whenever 'any subject concerning Jewish emancipation' was under discussion.

At their protest meeting Melbourne Jews gave full vent to their indignation at the decision of the legislature.[41] Yet the bitter mood and aggressive tone of the meeting cannot be explained solely by reference to local events in Victoria. It is better understood against the background of the drastic deterioration of the Jewish position in Europe in the wake of the post-1848 reaction, when many achievements of Jewish emancipation were undone. The *Jewish Chronicle* thus summed up the Jewish position on 3 February 1854:

> Our brethren of Rome, of Russia, of Austria, of Prussia, of Bavaria and Germany generally, of Italy, of Spain, of Portugal, of Turkey and of Barbary, are groaning under cruel arbitrary laws, and experiencing unmerited and unjust persecution.[42]

This was probably in the mind of the first speaker at the Melbourne meeting. 'There was equality in this country,' said A. H. Hart, 'although all around a spirit would walk to oppress them.' He called upon Jews to fight for their rights, for they 'must be indeed cowards if they did not show they had some of the blood of the Maccabees within them'.

There was a painful awareness that this latest blow was different in kind from previous adverse votes. As the Rev. Moses Rintel complained:

> Only a few years ago, when the Council had been applied to for a similar purpose, they were told it was to be regretted, but that the Constitution forbade it. Now they had the opportunity afforded of doing the Jews justice, what did they do? Why, by a majority they excluded them.

or as Michael Cashmore observed:

> The vote which had passed the Council was worthy of the antipodes where everything was contrary. In the old country every attempt was being made to sweep such unnatural prejudices away, but the first act of the Legislature of Victoria was to put among the laws everything which other countries were attempting to remove.

Cashmore gave vent to his urban and Jewish resentment against the group of elected conservative pastoralists or 'squatting' members in the Legislative Council (W. F. Splatt, W. Campbell, C. J. Griffith, J. Goodman, W. T. Mollison) who spoke and voted against the Jewish claim: 'Some members of the Council had not souls above *mutton*; others might take a higher flight, and ascend to wool, but that was the highest point to which they could soar.' In a similar vein Dr S. Iffla, a surgeon and the congregation's expert on education, denounced the Legislative Council for the 'injustice perpetrated against the Jewish body' and saw it arising 'from the leaven of deeply rooted prejudice which has been the foullest blot in the character of the otherwise liberal and enlightened people of Great Britain'. But he was sure that the 'spirit of intolerance' against them which had been revived in the Council would not take root 'in this colony'.

Apart from resenting the Legislative Council vote, Jews seem to have been stung by the tenor of the debate that preceded it. A resolution moved by the Rev. Moses Rintel protested against

> the attempt to throw ignominy and contempt on our sacred religion, which was the religion also of Moses, of Jesus and his disciples, by constantly placing at their side the Thugs, Hindoos and other such

abominations, is unjust, ungenerous, and far below the dignity that should characterise the proceedings of a British Legislative Assembly.

At the meeting it was decided to petition the Legislative Council. The Petition was nothing less than a remonstrance. It indignantly rejected such terms as 'toleration' and 'gratuity' which had been bandied about in the Legislative Council. It bore 504 signatures and read:

> Your Petitioners learn that in the proposed Constitution Bill about to be passed by Your Honourable House, a clause appropriating the sum of £50,000 to the support of Religion in this city has been introduced. Your Petitioners would view it as an insult to them were they to be excluded from a participation in such Grant.
>
> Your Petitioners are of opinion that it is oppressive in public as in private life to exclude one member from participation with the rest in the advantages to be derived from a general fund to which all contribute alike; and Your Petitioners only ask for themselves what they are desirous to concede to all.
>
> And while Your Petitioners ask neither for toleration in a Colony where all Her Majesty's subjects are upon an equality, nor favour from those who are bound to mete out justice to all, they claim as a right, being good citizens and loyal subjects, that they be not excluded from participation in the said Grant of £50,000 or that they be not compelled to bear an equal burden in the State with the recipients of such Grant. Your Petitioners therefore pray that Your Honourable Council before finally passing the New Constitution Bill, will place them upon terms of perfect Religious equality with all other classes of Her Majesty's subjects in Victoria.[43]

John O'Shanassy, the leader of the Irish Catholics in Victoria, presented the Jewish Petition in the Legislative Council on 17 March 1854. He moved that the word 'Christian' be struck out from the Public Worship clause.[44] John Myles, an extreme abolitionist, promptly moved that the clause be struck out altogether, and state aid be abolished. Myles's amendment was put first and defeated by 21 to 6 votes, showing that abolitionism in 1854 was at its nadir. O'Shanassy's motion that 'Christian' be struck out was defeated by 16 to 12 votes. J. P. Fawkner then tried again 'for his friends, the Hebrews' as the *Argus* put it, and moved that the word 'Hebrew' be added to the word 'Christian'. The debate which followed upon Fawkner's motion was not very different in substance from the February debate but its general tone was more embittered and outspoken.

T. T. à Beckett 'could not consider any religion to be a religion except the Christian religion'. It is true, they received the Jews' Bible, but 'the Jews felt the greatest contempt for Christians. He knew even Jews who would spit when Christians were mentioned'. He could not see how 'Christian legislators' could vote money for the support of the Jewish faith, a religion which was 'antagonistic to Christianity'. In a similar vein, John Myles, the Geelong demo-crat, urged that 'the Jewish religion must be a wrong religion if the Christian religion was a right one'. He tried the smear-tactics of some of the opponents of Jewish emancipation 'at home' by casting doubts on the bona fide character of the pro-Jewish vote: 'He wondered what penance would be inflicted upon Honourable Members for their vote. He thought that there was a great want of spirituality in discussing the matter.' This drew an angry retort from O'Shanassy, who called him a 'bigot' and added for good measure—'if there was a man that he had contempt for, it was a picaninny bigot.'

True to the spirit of his hero O'Connell and the Irish-Catholic tradition in the British House of Commons,[45] O'Shanassy pledged the support of the Catholics of Victoria to the Jewish aspirations for equality, who 'had learned by their own experience of persecu-tion to sympathise with those still suffering under persecution'. Such Catholic support of Jewish claims to state aid was not likely to cut much ice with Protestant Christian-state men who also be-lieved in an established church. These may not have had much more regard for Catholics and their 'Satanic delusion' than for 'blasphemous' Jews. If their opinions were to be swayed at all, it was rather in favour of the total abolition of state aid than its wider extension. The Collector of Customs (Childers) told those who had made great play with the Christian character of the legis-lature, that the fact of all its members being Christian, was mere accident: 'It only happened to be so but there was nothing to hinder the Jew from entering that House. They were all equal in the eyes of the law.'

Fawkner's amendment was defeated by 15 votes to 12. Though T. T. à Beckett must have been pleased by this second salvation of the Christian state, his incautious remarks in the debate earned him trouble. Three days later on 20 March many bankers and traders attended a farewell banquet to David Benjamin, a promin-ent Jewish leader and wealthy merchant and banker, who was returning to London. The Mayor of Melbourne, A. Hodgson, toasted Jacob Montefiore (who since 1852 was in Melbourne buy-ing gold and representing the Rothschilds) 'representing as he did the monied interests of Great Britain'. Montefiore in his reply paid tribute to the effacement of sectarian divisions and the integrative relations typical of the new colony:

> It gives me great pleasure to look round this numerous party and find men of every creed assembled to do honor to our friend Mr. David Benjamin. I can observe sitting at this table the Protestant, the Catholic and the Unitarian all assembled to do honor to the Jew and without fear of contamination or of being spit upon as was observed the other day in the Legislative Council Chambers by Mr. à Beckett.[46]

These remarks provoked à Beckett to write to the *Melbourne Morning Herald*: his speech in the Legislative Council had been mis-interpreted and his opposition to Jewish participation in state aid derived from principle and not from prejudice. He ended on an apologetic note:

> I believe there is no one who respects the Jewish people more or regards them as a nation with a higher feeling than I do. I am therefore anxious that my vote on the last debate in which they were interested, should be placed upon its real grounds.[47]

Melbourne Jews did not believe him nor did they accept his 'endeavours to palliate his conduct . . . in his gratuitous calumny against the Jews as a body' as one of a series of letters published in the *Melbourne Morning Herald* put it. They felt that his 'calumniating remarks' were meant to 'strengthen his opposition to a just right due to the Jews as citizens and loyal subjects'.[48] Whatever the importance of the banquet and the à Beckett incident, it affords some insight into the social climate of mid-nineteenth-century Victoria as it affected Jews.

The Victorian legislature had now twice, and independently from Colonial Office instruction or New South Wales precedent, decided not to recognize the religious existence of Victorian Jews in the new constitution. But the Jews were not ready to give up. They need not regard the vote 'against them' as representative of the real feelings and opinions of the colony. The squatters and their conservative allies were still overrepresented in the legislature and the 'back-the-Church' movement, which the panic of the gold-rushes had touched off, was at its peak.[49]

The Jews began by addressing the new Lieutenant-Governor, Sir Charles Hotham. Hotham seems to have assured them 'heart and soul he was in favour of perfect civil and religious liberty'.[50] But whatever he may have thought of the Christian definition of the

Public Worship clause, he had no power to intervene against a majority decision of the Legislative Council.

The British Parliament had postponed consideration of the New Constitution Bill. Voluntaryists in the colony were petitioning the Queen to abolish the Public Worship clause,[51] and Melbourne Jews now petitioned her to insert the words 'and Hebrew persuasion', in the clause.[52] The Petition recalled that Jews had been among the earliest settlers in the colony, and their number was now 'upwards of Five thousand'.[53] Among them were to be found 'persons of all grades and classes of society, Members of eminent Mercantile Houses, wealthy proprietors and many devoted to scientific and literary pursuits'. Thus in addition to their being 'large contributors' to the general revenue they also 'materially aid in the moral, social and physical advancement of the Colony'. They had full political rights and like Jews in all British colonies, they were 'eligible to sit and vote as Members of the Legislative Council'. In the past, land had been granted to them for 'religious purposes'. However, the New Constitution Bill would exclude their religion from participation in state aid though their right to participate in state aid had been 'strongly urged' when the Bill was before the Legislative Council and was only negatived by a 'bare majority of one vote and that in consequence of the unavoidable absence of three representative members.' They were not actuated by any 'mercenary motive' but wished only to appeal against an act of 'manifest injustice' for 'as they are represented in all matters in the same manner as the rest of Your Majesty's subjects any attempt to separate Legislation for them is unjust and improper.'

The Petition reached the Colonial Office on 17 March 1855. Herman Merivale, the Permanent Under-Secretary who minuted it, thought it unlikely that Parliament would 'make any such amendment' as Melbourne Jews had asked for.[54] In the very act of granting responsible government, neither Parliament nor the Colonial Office was likely to reverse a decision of the Victorian legislature. But if that decision was to exclude Jews from state aid, at least the Colonial Office under Lord John Russell need not help it along. Russell's despatch to Governor Hotham shows that, in the existing situation, this champion of Jewish emancipation in England did all he could to assist the cause in Victoria. He instructed Hotham to let the petitioners know that their Petition could not be acceded to. But he also made it clear that he hoped the Victorian legislature would change its mind: 'The wishes of the colony, however, should they propose to admit the Jews to participate in the funds for Public Worship, will receive a favourable attention.'[55]

There were other causes for hope. English Jews applauded the determined spirit of their Melbourne brethren. An editorial in the *Jewish Chronicle*, published just after Russell's Oath Bill had been defeated, held up Melbourne Jews as an example to English Jews, who were reminded 'how energetically the Jews in Melbourne have recently met and protested against threatening intolerance and oppression on the part of the local legislature.'[56]

Closer to home, liberal opinion in the colony was on their side. The influential *Argus* 'utterly disapproved' of the 'Christian limitation' of the Public Worship clause,[57] and a majority of 'liberal' members in the Legislative Council consistently supported the Jewish cause.[58] Moreover, the very constitution which in its Public Worship clause (no. 53) refused to recognize the religious equality of the Jew, provided in its electoral clause (no. 12) for a very wide suffrage. The conservative phalanx of nominee and squatter would soon be outvoted by a more liberal and representative majority. At the farewell dinner to David Benjamin, the banker A. H. Smith responded thus to a toast to the 'commercial interests' of Victoria: 'the day was past when the squatters played first fiddle, they were nowhere now—their sun had set.'[59] The liberal democracy could be expected to give Jews religious equality before abolishing state aid.

9

Liberalism Triumphant in Victoria 1856-1859

When in September 1855 Melbourne Jews learned that their Petition to the Queen had been unsuccessful,[1] they recognized the failure of their last and somewhat pathetic attempt to prevent a Christian definition of public worship from being written into the new constitution. At the same time, some abolitionists tried to prevent the implementation of the 53rd clause until after the first general election under the new constitution; that effort also failed.[2]

In addition to the principle of religious equality for which they had been fighting, Melbourne Jews had now a cogent material reason for continuing to press for state aid. They owed £2,500 for the new synagogue.[3] At the height of the gold rushes many fine churches and chapels were built; the Jews felt compelled to join in this extravagance 'to meet the growing wants of our co-religionists in order that it may no longer be a reflection on this important congregation that she is so far behind her neighbours of other denominations.'[4] So they built on the same scale, but without the handsome building grants which their neighbours got from the Christian state. An economic crisis hit the colony at the end of 1854. Among the worst affected were city merchants, wholesalers, warehouse-owners, auctioneers and shopkeepers, the commercial ranks in which Melbourne Jews were so well represented.[5] One purpose of the big synagogue was to provide for the needs of a big immigration, but too many of the newcomers proved unappreciative. One reason for their much denounced and lamented apathy[6] seems to have been the oligarchical structure of the Melbourne Hebrew Congregation. Only 'privileged members' as distinct from mere 'seat-holders' had the full franchise and right to synagogual 'honours', while admission to privileged membership was selective and costly (it was raised to five guineas in 1852). One protest letter

signed by 'One of Yourselves' demanded that the struggle for
Jewish equality be carried also into the synagogue: 'Remember
our brethren are asking from other creeds what they positively
deny *in toto* to their own body, viz. Civil and Religious Liberty.'[7]

On 3 February 1856 the congregational authorities applied to the
colonial government for a special grant of £2,500 'to enable the
Hebrews of Melbourne to complete their House of Prayer'. It was
under 'most urgent circumstances', wrote Edward Cohen, President of the Melbourne Congregation, to W. C. Haines, the Chief
Secretary, that they asked for that aid, not out of the 53rd clause
'that we know we are shut out from', but from the estimates.[8]
Haines suggested that they wait until the new legislature had
been elected when they 'may very properly demand' that their
claim be considered.[9]

In the 1856 election campaign state aid to religion in general and
the Public Worship clause in particular were major issues.[10] Prac-
tically all candidates had to declare themselves for or against state
aid.[11] As J. S. Gregory has shown, opposition to state aid went
hand in hand with 'support for the democratic programme of
political reform' and became one of the main planks in the platform
of what the *Melbourne Morning Herald* called 'the liberal party',
whereas conservative candidates defended the retention of state
aid.[12] From our point of view the 1856 election campaign is of
special interest in so far as it marked a turning-point in the
attitudes of some leading Christian-state men to the Jewish
'question'.

By 1856 'liberalism' had become a catchword in the colony. Even
'a Tory to the backbone'[13] like R. W. Pohlman felt he must describe
himself as a 'liberal conservative',[14] and conservative supporters of
state aid were clearly on the defensive. They found it particularly
difficult to counter the liberal-democratic argument that the Public
Worship clause was 'illiberal' and 'unjust' because one section of
the community, the Jews, were deliberately excluded from it.[15]
Whatever their motives, diehard Christian-state men like T. T.
à Beckett and R. W. Pohlman, J. F. L. Foster, John Goodman and
W. F. Stawell, rediscovered in 1856 and 1857 the Jewish ancestry of
Christianity and made it publicly known they had changed their
mind and would now extend state aid to Jews. This volte-face
was not unduly surprising; there were more than local reasons for
it. Russell's despatches of 21 May 1855 to the governors of New
South Wales, Tasmania and Victoria had been unambiguous indi-
cations of a drastic change in Colonial Office policy. Grey's veto

had been lifted; decisions by colonial legislatures to admit the Jewish religion to state aid would receive the blessings of the Secretary of State. Moreover, both New South Wales and Van Diemen's Land had shown the way when in September 1855 they granted state aid to their Jews.

In the light of the uncompromising stand Pohlman and à Beckett had taken on the Jewish question in the Legislative Council in previous years, the views they expressed in the course of the 1856 election campaign deserve special attention. They still believed in the religious duties of the state,[16] so they could not use the expedient secular argument that 'religion was the cheapest police'.[17] They wanted to continue state aid, but they had to cope with the democratic-voluntaryist argument which in the name of equality tried to make state aid absurd by demanding its indiscriminate extension to all religion—in the needling words of the anti-clerical Dr Thomas Embling, 'to the rabbis of Israel, the brahmins of Hindooism, the priests of Zoroaster, the disciples of Socinius and Confucius, and the followers of Joe Smith.'[18] So it was to draw the line *somewhere* that Pohlman and à Beckett suddenly seized on the Jewish ancestry of Christianity and on the Bible as the foundation common to both. Pohlman confessed he had some difficulty 'to reconcile the bounty to the members of the Jewish persuasion'. He managed somehow—and 'caused a sensation' when he of all people now favoured state aid to the Jewish religion because 'Judaism was Christianity begun and Christianity is Judaism finished'.[19]

à Beckett too did not find it 'pleasant' to admit 'an error in judgment', and it was only 'after very much consideration' he also changed his mind. In March 1854 the Jewish religion had seemed 'antagonistic to Christianity'. Now he pleaded 'the right of the Jew' to participate in state aid on the ground that 'the religion of the Jew . . . is the very foundation of the Christian faith . . . founded on the Old Testament Scriptures cannot but be acceptable to the Almighty'. Besides some state aid, it was also 'the duty of the Christians of the present day to honour the Jewish nation as that people to whom were committed the oracles of God; as the natural olive tree on which we, representing the wild olive tree, have been grafted.'[20]

If Pohlman and à Beckett, probably the most consistent and vociferous opponents of Jewish religious equality in the old Legislative Council, had recanted in 1856, so did the architect of the Christian definition of the Public Worship clause, J. F. L. Foster, and also

H

John Goodman, a leading squatter and diehard conservative. Foster's 'broad line of demarcation' between Christianity and Judaism of February 1852 seems to have faded, enough to allow him to say that

> he had altered in one point—and that was in his opinion of the propriety of introducing the word 'Christian' into the Constitution Act. He now saw no reason why the word 'Hebrew' should not also be there. He thought a portion of the aid should also be assigned to the Jews. He was then wrong. Now he thought differently. Although the Jews did not believe exactly the same as ourselves, their morality was based on the same scriptures as was ours . . .[21]

A similar declaration by Goodman that he would now 'support a proposition that the Jews should receive a fair share' of state aid was greeted with 'cheers'.[22] These public exercises of the conscience of the Christian state must have occasioned some wry amusement—as well as political satisfaction—to the Jewish community in Victoria.

Melbourne Jews, however, were not passive celebrants of this change of climate. At many meetings in 1856 they were active in support of a large variety of candidates, ranging from outright abolitionists to repentant Christian-state men like à Beckett and W. F. Stawell.[23] Most of their support went to abolitionist candidates like David Moore or John Hood,[24] or to a 'champion of civil and religious liberty' like John O'Shanassy.[25] But Michael Cashmore, a very prominent Jewish leader, proposed Stawell as a 'fit and proper person to represent the city of Melbourne in the Legislative Assembly' and made a long speech on his behalf.[26] As the best irony of all, one called Nathaniel Levy did the same service for à Beckett and amidst 'groans and cheers' and calls of 'what has he paid you?' proposed him as a 'fit and proper person' and praised him as a 'man of intellect and a practical statesman'.[27] On the central working committee for the return of à Beckett we find, as well as Levy, Samuel Cohen and A. Henriques, 'practical statesmen' too.[28] Whatever interpretation we put on this unexpected Jewish patronage of à Beckett and Stawell, it suggests that Melbourne Jews were at work to widen *any* breach in the wall of the Christian state.

In the new Legislative Assembly after the 1856 elections, liberals and abolitionists were in a clear majority. Progress towards complete religious equality began in June 1857 with Archibald Michie's Abolition Bill.[29] This would have abolished state aid to religion after 31 December 1859, and it promised the Jews 'a fair proportion' of state aid in the interim. During the debate only one diehard, C. F. Griffith, remained to uphold the principle of the Christian state and 'the supposition that we were a Christian people'. He opposed state aid to Jews on the ground that

> it would be the height of inconsistency to pay men for teaching doctrines which, if they were published, might subject the publishers to a prosecution for blasphemy. (No, No.) Every conscientious Jew held the founder of our religion to have been an impostor, and if this were published for general circulation, it would amount to what every man, or at least every Christian, must consider blasphemy.[30]

However, in the Legislative Assembly of 1857 Griffith's was a lone voice and a majority of members were determined to avoid that 'inconsistency' which state aid in a multi-denominational and democratic society was bound to produce. It was not the extreme Tory squatter Griffith, but a new member, the Quaker democrat Charles Read, who expressed the opinion of the majority when he urged that 'the best thing for any Legislature to do for religion was to let it alone—neither pamper nor persecute it'.[31]

Though the Assembly passed this Abolition Bill comfortably at its first and second readings (38 to 23 and 32 to 20), it was defeated in the upper house.[32] The 53rd clause was part of the new constitution and could only be repealed by absolute majorities in both houses. But the conservative Legislative Council could not prevent the enactment of two new measures which arose out of the Michie Abolition Bill, the Oaths of Office Simplification Bill of 1857 and the grant in aid of the 'Jewish Community, Victoria' in February 1859. The Oaths of Office Simplification Bill,[33] like a similar New South Wales measure of 1856, did away with the oaths of allegiance, supremacy and abjuration and replaced all three with one oath of allegiance whose terms offered no offence to Jew, Catholic or Protestant. In the colony of Victoria no Jew had yet been elected to the legislature so none had been asked to take the oath of abjuration 'on the true faith of a Christian'. Archibald Michie, a liberal abolitionist who moved the new Bill, made clear its intention 'to repeal that Oath affecting persons of the Jewish persuasion—the Oath which prevented Mr. Salomons taking his seat in the House of Commons when returned for London, because he would not take an oath ending with the words "on the true faith of a Christian." '[34]

This Victorian Act was interesting, and in the Australian colonies unusual, in that its preamble included a positive declaration of the principle of religious equality: 'the civil and religious liberties of Her Majesty's subjects are and ought to be equal irrespective of their faith or form of belief'.[35] Before that fundamental declaration Christian denominations in the colony had enjoyed a merely *de facto* equality, inasmuch as the Bourke Church Act and then the Public Worship Clause of the new constitution had allowed them equal access to state aid. For some of them, that was a reason for continuing state aid, in the absence of any other demonstration of their equality. Thus when the abolitionism was gaining wider and wider support in the colony in 1856 and 1857, even liberal Catholics like O'Shanassy favoured the retention of state aid, as they felt that their religious equality was vested in their receiving an equal share in state aid. Their fears were reasonable at a time when the Churches of England and Scotland were established 'at home', and Anglo-Irish Anglicans were prominent in colonial government. As O'Shanassy put it in December 1855 when attacking Dr Embling's move to prevent implementation of the 53rd clause:

> On the ground of perfect religious equality it was that he opposed the voluntary principle, for withdraw existing laws, and the country would be plunged at once into sectarian discord, and it would soon be found that certain gentlemen would try to make themselves into the dominant Church. This they never could do whilst there was that great fundamental landmark in their Constitution, the Act of Sir Richard Bourke, in existence to prevent it, and never would he consent to having that Act withdrawn until it could be satisfactorily replaced by something else.[36]

The preamble of the Oaths of Office Simplification Bill was precisely that 'something else', a charter to replace 'equal state aid' as a reassurance to O'Shanassy and the Catholics in general.[37]

For the Jews in Victoria it seems to have done more than that. Instead of merely replacing 'equal state aid' it promised the end of *unequal* aid, and of the Christian state which the inequality symbolized. The promise was still, however, entangled in an outstanding contradiction. The 53rd clause of the constitution still discriminated against Jews and other non-Christians, while the preamble of the Oaths of Office Simplification Act affirmed the religious equality of Christian, Jew and possibly pagan, and by implication recognized the Jewish claim to state aid. A practical equality, if not a perfect one in principle, was achieved when James Service, a liberal Scot and a merchant, on 8 February 1859 moved in the Legislative Assembly for a grant 'in aid of the funds of the Jewish Community, Victoria'. 'All he sought was to obtain for the members of the Jewish persuasion a recognition of their civil rights'.[38] The motion was opposed on various grounds but only Colin Campbell, conservative squatter, champion of church schools and future parson, spoke up for the Christian state and declared that 'He was not prepared to support any grant which extended equal advantages to a creed which they supported as true and one which they believed in error'.[39] Any other opposition was not anti-equalitarian; it came from extreme voluntaryists like George Harker and John Myles. Myles, a voluntaryist but probably anti-Catholic and a Christian-state man into the bargain, 'regretted that there was such a sad defection on the part of many hon. members, who had heretofore opposed to state aid'.[40] It was a large defection; as usual, most voluntaryists were also staunch believers in religious equality. The advanced liberal and social reformer Richard Heales expressed their point of view admirably: 'As a voluntary he was opposed to any increase in the amount in support of State endowment, but was still more opposed to anything like religious persecution.'[41]

Service's motion was passed 28 to 11. The eleven opponents included conservative Christian-state men like Rutledge, Mollison and Colin Campbell, and extreme voluntaryists like Harker, Myles and James Henty.[42] Thus by an overwhelming majority the Victorian Legislative Assembly at last recognized the religious equality of the Jew in the colony and his claim to state aid. If the grant still had to come from general revenue instead of from the public worship fund, it was nevertheless well known that the Assembly would have revised or abolished the Public Worship clause, too, if the conservative upper house had allowed it.

'In aid of the funds of the Jewish Community', £2,000 was granted annually until 1862, then £500 until state aid was abolished altogether in 1872.[43] It is reasonable to regard those grants as marking the achievement of Jewish religious equality in Victoria. Equality in education followed, when in 1859 £310 was allocated by the Denominational Board of Education towards Jewish denominational education, and the merchant Isaac Hart was admitted to the Board as representative of the Jewish community.[44]

The significance of the struggle for equality was not lost on one group of Jews who were, perforce, only spectators of it. On 27 February 1859, a couple of weeks after the success of Service's motion, six Jewish prisoners in Pentridge Stockade appealed to Michael Cashmore, President of the Melbourne Hebrew Congregation, to help persuade the prison authorities that Jewish prisoners should be exempted from work to celebrate the Jewish festivals. George Aaron, their spokesman, aimed straight at the soft spots of his brethren 'outside'; 'I think it would be both right and proper for the Jewish persuasion to receive the same privileges as regards their religious observances as other sects in Bondage as well as at Freedom.'[45] By 1859 even the jailbirds had mastered the language of Jewish emancipation.

If one compares the fate of the Jewish struggle for equal religious rights in Victoria, at least during its decisive phase in 1853–5, with what happened in the other colonies, there appears a certain fundamental difference, both in the course of events and in their 'temperature'. The legislatures of South Australia, New South Wales and Van Diemen's Land, whenever the question of state aid to the Jewish religion was discussed, had generally favoured aid. Any serious opposition to Jewish religious equality came from governors, and from the Colonial Office—from Franklin and Eardley-Wilmot in Van Diemen's Land, Gipps in New South Wales, Stanley, Gladstone, James Stephen and above all Earl Grey at the Colonial Office. Even the exceptional cases, the defeat of Wentworth's Church Act Amendment Bill in 1849 and the 'draw' of 1853 in New South Wales, were due mainly to the reluctance of government members of the legislatures to displease Grey. Thus the colonial will, in so far as it found expression in the Legislative Councils and in the press of South Australia, New South Wales and Van Diemen's Land, favoured Jewish equality in principle, though it was often enough thwarted in action.

In Victoria in 1853 and 1854 the Legislative Council was free to legislate as it liked on state aid to religion. It decided repeatedly to exclude Jews from that aid, and even entrenched the exclusion in the new constitution. Thus Jews in Victoria found themselves in the pathetic position of protesting to the Secretary of State against discrimination by their own colonial legislature. The reason for this striking difference may possibly be that in none of the other colonies were the champions of the Jewish cause so closely identified with a liberal-popular, anti-squatting 'party' as in Victoria: it almost assumed the character of a minor issue in a larger conflict between aggressive liberals and defensive but well entrenched conservatives.

In South Australia, it is safe to say, there never was a Jewish problem. In Van Diemen's Land when it arose in the early 1850s, the liberal anti-transportationists had already won, and monopolized the two-thirds elected majority in the Legislative Council. In New South Wales until 1853 W. C. Wentworth, the leader of the squatters, was the chief champion of the Jewish cause in the Legislative Council. Yet he was seconded by anti-squatting liberals and radicals like Robert Lowe, J. D. Lang and G. R. Nichols. Both Wentworth and Dr H. G. Douglass in 1853, as well as Nichols in 1854, could and did, when championing Jewish equality, appeal to sentiments of colonial independence against 'dictation' by Earl Grey. In 1845, 1846 and 1854 they carried with them a majority of the members of the Legislative Council, whatever their social and political ties, to vote in favour of their Jews.

In Victoria, however, as A. H. Hart observed 'there were two parties in the house, one for them and one against them':[46] whenever the question of the extension of state aid to Jews arose in the Legislative Council, it was consistently opposed by a solid core of conservative government officials, nominees and squatters.[47] Just as invariably did elected members with a clear liberal-radical outlook and a strong anti-squatting reputation—J. P. Fawkner and William Westgarth, J. S. Johnston and Henry Miller, J. T. Smith and John O'Shanassy—take up and champion the cause of the Victorian Jewish community. It is almost symbolic that on the very days (16 February and 17 March 1854) that Fawkner moved for 'his friends the Hebrews', he also delivered broadsides against his 'enemies' the squatters.[48]

Neither Fawkner, the irreconcilable fighter 'against all squatterdom' nor O'Shanassy, the Irish-Catholic draper with a similar anti-squatting and radical record,[49] was likely to succeed in 1854 where the universally respected and prudent Westgarth had failed in 1852, namely, in swaying the opinions and votes of 'episcopalian' Christian-state men like T. T. à Beckett, R. W. Pohlman and C. J. Griffith; conservative and staunchly Anglican government officials like J. F. L. Foster and W. F. Stawell; conservative squatters like W. F. Splatt, John Goodman, W. T. Mollison, William Campbell and J. C. Riddell. In February and March 1854 these conservatives combined with a few extreme abolitionists like John Myles, James Cowie and J. T. Charlton and a 'conservative liberal' and Christian-state man like J. F. Strachan,[50] to exclude Jews from the Public Worship clause of the New Constitution and thus to preserve the Christian state in Victoria.

Conclusion

This study began by suggesting that the Jewish agitation for an equitable share in state aid to religion was the peculiarly Australian form of a world-wide movement for Jewish emancipation. It is time now to ask how it compared with the Jewish struggle in Europe, especially in England, and what was perculiarly 'Australian' about it?

In the first place it appears that Australian Jews hardly ever resorted to the supplicant lobbying tactics which marked the early stages of the Jewish emancipation movement in the 'old world'. There—to the dismay of Jewish liberals—wealthy and influential Jewish bankers like the Rothschilds, in the tradition of the Court Jews of the seventeenth and eighteenth centuries, interceded with the mighty of Europe for partial concessions; they even begged favours of conservatives and reactionaries like Count Metternich and the Duke of Wellington.[1] Moses Montefiore's diary records Nathan Mayer Rothschild's obsequious plea to the Duke of Wellington in 1830: 'God has given your grace power, said Rothschild, I would entreat you to do something for the Jews.'[2] It is true that Australian Jews often asked Sir Moses Montefiore to 'intercede' on their behalf with the Colonial Office. But he was the President of the Board of Deputies of British Jews and it was in that public and official capacity that his Australian brethren approached him, and he in turn approached the Secretary of State for the Colonies.

Jews in Australia campaigned collectively as an organized group in full daylight, if not limelight, through official channels, the colonial legislatures and the press. Their main instrument was not the discreet plea of a Jewish banker in high places, but rather the Petition which was published in the press and read in the legislature. Their policies were clearly identified with colonial liberal-

ism. Both the Jewish and the Christian champions of their cause
were liberals to a man. Nor did Australian Jews stoop to 'entreat'
the legislatures or the governors 'to do something for the Jews' as a
'gratuity' or 'favour' but rather claimed a share in state aid as a
right, the right of citizens who contributed equally with others
to the prosperity of the state. The Melbourne Jewish Petition to
the Legislative Council of Victoria in February 1854, perhaps more
militant and aggressive in tone than most, was still in essence
typical. Melbourne Jews, it said,

> ask neither for toleration in a Colony where all Her Majesty's subjects
> are upon an equality, nor favour from those who are bound to mete
> out justice to all; they claim as a right, being good citizens and loyal
> subjects, that they be not excluded from participation in . . . state
> aid . . . or that they be not compelled to bear an equal burden in the
> State with the recipients of such Grant . . . [3]

One characteristic feature of the emancipation movement in
France, Germany and, to a lesser extent, in England, was the pro-
fession of Jews, in season and out, of their full identification with
the nation amidst whom they lived. They claimed to be nothing
but Frenchmen, Germans, Englishmen who just happened to be
of the 'Mosaic' persuasion; there was no 'Jewish nation' and they
did not belong to one. The Assembly of Jewish Notables which
Napoleon convoked in 1806 proclaimed: 'Now that the privilege
was granted to us to be accepted into a great French nation, we
Jews have ceased to form a nation and we regard this as our
political deliverance.'[4] Even as proud a Jew and as relentless a
fighter for emancipation as Gabriel Riesser was in Germany,
emphatically denied the existence of a 'Jewish nation' which, he
believed, had ceased to exist 'since the bastions of Jerusalem fell
and the people of Judea were dispersed all over the Roman Empire'; he urged that German Jews were nothing but 'a group of
people who do not wish to have a national existence of their own,
such as had formerly been imposed upon them by their enemies,
but who think and feel as Germans.'[5] When in the House of Commons the term 'Jewish nation' had been much bandied about by
the opponents of emancipation, a Jewish spokesmen and pam-
phleteer, Dr Barnard van Oven, felt he

> must protest at once against the employment of the term nation.
> There is no such thing, as the Jewish nation. It is long since the Jews
> have ceased to be a nation and have been (in the words of the sacred
> Scriptures) scattered amongst the nations of the earth.[6]

Australian Jews in the 1840s and 1850s did and said nothing of this sort. Perhaps because their Australian loyalty was rarely challenged, they saw no need to renounce any other loyalty. They did use the term 'Jewish nation' from time to time on specially solemn occasions, both private and public. Early in 1843, various Jewish congregations were thanked for contributing to the cost of the Sydney synagogue, 'the first place of public worship for the Hebrew nation in the Southern Hemisphere'.[7] In 1839 George Moss, the honorary secretary of the Sydney Hebrew Congregation, begged its committee to have his bride made a proselyte, so that his 'intended marriage should be agreeably to the rites and customs of the Hebrew Nation',[8] while the earliest Jewish catechism published in Sydney in 1855, the Rev. M. R. Cohen's *Principles of Judaism . . . for the Use of Scholars of Zion House*, professed as its object 'the instruction of the Hebrew youth in the principles of their national faith'.[9] At the anniversary dinner of the consecration of the Sydney synagogue in April 1845, Moss toasted the 'health of Sir Moses Montefiore' *and* of 'the Jewish Nation' and spoke then of 'the rise and fall of the children of Israel, and the fierce persecution to which they have in successive ages been exposed . . . the vile Damascus charge—the Ancona decree—the Russian Autocrat's Deportation Ukase—and the recent atrocities at Mogador.'[10] He thus underlined the solidarity of Australian Jews with their oppressed brethren in the near east, Switzerland, Russia and Morocco and anywhere in the world, and felt they belonged to the same 'Jewish nation'. That solidarity with a Jewish nation was also the theme of P. J. Cohen, the founder of organized Jewish life in Australia, when at a public meeting in Sydney on 8 November 1858 he celebrated the Jews' Relief Act:

> they ought not to forget the cause of their brethren in other parts of the world—for though widely separated as individuals, they were all members of one nation, united in the bonds of brotherhood and while successful themselves, they must endeavour to loosen the bonds in which the Jews in other countries were politically enthralled, so as to place them on a par with their fellow-subjects.[11]

The same difference in attitude between timid 'old world' Jews and their confident colonial brethren can be discerned in one exchange of sentiments in the 1850s. The Rev. Herman Hoelzel applied from London in 1852 for the position of rabbi of the Sydney Hebrew Congregation. His letter of application may be compared with the address of welcome he received when at long last he reached Sydney in 1856 to take up his post. He promised this:

> I shall strive, with the blessings of Divine Providence, to render
> Judaism respected and esteemed in the great world of the South, by
> proving that while it conducts its votaries on the path of virtue, it is in
> no wise incompatible with the cultivation of those social relations
> between man and man which are the bonds of peace, goodwill and
> brotherhood among the members of all creeds and the denizens of
> all kinds—alike the children of One Almighty Father. . . .[12]

His employers, the Sydney Jews, welcomed him thus:

> we cannot allow so important an event in the history of our nation in
> this colony to be hurried past, without recording the grateful feelings
> of this community to that Divine Providence which has never yet
> deserted the flock of Israel . . . whilst we call upon you to uphold the
> ancient landmarks of Israel, we ask you to observe with sincerity,
> that we are not unmindful of the progress and education in dispelling
> the impurities of obsolete religious ceremonies which can only trace
> their origin to the dispersion of our nation amongst the inhabitants of
> the earth.[13]

There is an air of ease and freedom about this evidence that
Jews in the Australian colonies felt they could afford to be true to
themselves, and appear in private and in public as what they were:
bona fide settlers and members of the colonial society in which
they had made their home, yet possessed of a high degree of
religious, social and cultural identification with a dispersed 'Jewish
nation'.

Another comparison, of more portentous utterances, is just as
telling. There were significant differences between the arguments
used by the opponents of Jewish political equality in England, and
the arguments used by the opponents of Jewish religious equality
in Australia.

When in the British Parliament men like Lord Stanley, the Arch-
bishop of Canterbury, or Sir Robert Inglis, the Tory member for
Oxford, spoke against Jewish emancipation they were rarely satisfied with the formal argument for the Christian state: 'Christianity
was part and parcel of the Laws of England' and Jews could therefore have no place in a Christian legislature. They improved that
simple theme with much embroidery. English Jews were 'aliens',
'strangers', 'temporary sojourners' in England, 'a nation apart', who
viewed Christ as 'an impostor and a blasphemer' and professed 'a
religion which was essentially and decidedly hostile to the faith of
Christ'.[14] From a House of Lords debate of 25 May 1848 Lord
Stanley may be quoted as perhaps the best but still a typical em-

broiderer: he believed that there could be no 'greater disqualifica-
tion in a Christian assembly and a Christian country—in a country
in which the law rests on the basis of Christianity—in which
Christianity is part and parcel of the law of the realm' than to be a
Jew and deny the truth of Christianity. Besides that greater dis-
qualification, there were also lesser ones: for example a Jew must
believe 'even the Second Person of the Blessed Trinity to be a convicted malefactor, and justly condemned by the law of an offended
country.' For another example,

> practically the Jews of this country are not of this country, but are a
> nation apart. As temporary sojourners within this country they are
> entitled to the hospitality and to the protection of this country, but
> they have no special British interests any more than special German
> interests or special French interests. They have the interests of the
> Jews at heart, not British interests, and above all, not Christian
> interests . . .

On these grounds Stanley felt he could not 'place the Jew, either
with regard to his religious belief or with regard to his social condition, on the footing of any denomination of Christians, nor can
he place him on the footing of other British subjects.'[15]

Stanley was not the worst. There were still a few who blamed
nineteenth-century British Jews for the crucifixion of Christ which
was 'the great national crime for which they were now suffering'
being 'under God's curse . . . suffering Divine Judgment'; or denounced them as people who 'never laboured' . . . 'were never seen
wielding the flail, or mounting the ladder with the hod' but were
'essentially traffickers in money'.[16]

Scarcely any of these arguments were ever heard in the Australian legislatures. There, the stock objections to state aid to
Jewish religion were that a Christian state must not assist a non-
Christian religion, or that aid to Jews would create a dangerous
precedent for aid to Hindus, Moslems and pagans. The argument
that Jews formed 'a nation apart' was only voiced once, by James
Martin in the Legislative Council of New South Wales;[17] that they
were 'antagonistic to Christianity' only by Sir John Franklin in Van
Diemen's Land, 'Christianus' in New South Wales, and C. J.
Griffith and T. T. à Beckett in Victoria.

In the Australian colonies even among the 'founding fathers'
Jews had found a place. A majority of colonists, whether Gentile
or Jew, bond or free, were immigrants: cries of 'alien' or 'temporary' would have seemed slightly absurd. The Jews who had settled

in Sydney, Adelaide, Hobart and Melbourne in the 1830s, 1840s and 1850s, did well for themselves and soon had a solid and obvious stake in the country. Most of them had originally come from England and were in language, dress and bearing hardly distinguishable from other members of the urban commercial class in the colonies, of which they formed quite a substantial section at a time when its wealth, prestige and influence was in the ascendant. Unlike their counterparts, the Jewish upper and middle classes in the larger cities of the 'old world' they were not embarrassed by any noticeable presence of exotic-looking and spiritually unemancipated arrivals from a recent Ghetto-environment.[18]

They waged their struggle for religious equality at a time when liberalism was the conquering ideology and in an environment which by and large seems to have approved of them and of their aspirations. A new, dynamic, money-making colonial society, characterized by an almost unprecedented 'political and social inclusiveness'[19] which refused to discriminate against former convicts, was not likely to harbour strong prejudices against a Montefiore, a Benjamin or a Cohen because he was a Jew. As John West, the historian of Van Diemen's Land, put it in 1852; 'the tendency of colonial life is to annul the prejudices of European society and to yield to every man the position which may be due to his talents or virtues'.[20] The general climate of opinion in the Australian colonies not only made for equality to the detriment of privilege; it positively encouraged people to be proud, stand up for themselves and assert their independence. As a young Jew put it in 1853 when giving an account of the 'new country' in a letter home: 'this is a country of plenty, and full of independence, for a man is here indeed a man'.[21] Australian Jews in their dignified determination displayed the kind of 'men' they were and reflected to some extent the ethos of the colonial society of which they formed part.

It is then the overall dignity, consistency and firmness of the Jewish struggle for religious equality in the Australian colonies, the absence of cringing and self-deprecation on the part of the Jewish communities, which strike one as the significant Australian peculiarity of this relatively minor incident in the history of the Jewish emancipation movement in the nineteenth century.

It seems reasonable to suggest that one result or by-product of the Jewish struggle for state aid was to assist the spread of the principle of religious equality in the Australian colonies and to promote its acceptance. Even if Jews did nothing more than demand a share in state aid, they and their champions did so in the name of religious equality. There were few debates in the Australian legislatures on the question of state aid to Jews, where the rights of all sects, even of pagans, to a share in state aid would not be mentioned, if not urged, by consistent liberals. The position of the less popular or more problematic Christian denominations, e.g. of Catholics or Unitarians, could only be strengthened when even Jews clamoured for equal religious rights. For if the claims of a non-Christian denomination were taken seriously, even when in the name of Christianity they were refused, the religious rights of all Christians became unassailable.

Generally it seems that the Jewish grievance furnished a concrete and live issue around which ideas of religious tolerance and equality could crystallize. It provided liberals and radicals with the opportunity to propagate their ideas of religious tolerance and liberty in the legislatures and in the press and to translate them into legislative action. Though the Oaths Bills in New South Wales and in Victoria which put the principle of religious equality into the statute-book were concessions chiefly to the susceptibilities of Catholics, the Jewish contribution towards them was to turn the question of religious equality into a real concrete issue which could not be ignored.

If the separation of state and church formed part of the liberal creed, Jewish claims to state aid often gave the creed some practical urgency, won it a few more allies, and thus helped on the progressive secularization of the Australian colonies. O'Shanassy had this in mind when in 1855 he reproached abolitionists for using the Jewish grievance as a 'handle' to discredit state aid to religion. T. T. à Beckett and William Rutledge in September 1852 accused Westgarth and Miller of having brought forward the motion for state aid to Jews chiefly in order 'to do away with the grant altogether'. Consistent Christian-state men would sooner abolish state aid altogether than allow Jews to participate in it. Archibald Michie, a late convert to abolitionism, may have had this in mind when he explained his vote in support of the grant to the Jewish community of Victoria: 'If the principle of State aid were a rotten one, it was by heaping extreme cases upon it that it would be borne down.'[22] Though Jews when fighting for state aid *eo ipso* also fought against the notion of the Christian state, they did not necessarily or consciously work for a secular state. All they did was to provide concrete and irksome evidence to those who held strong views as to the religious responsibilities of the state, that in a democratic and multi-denominational society 'the best thing', as

Charles Read put it in 1857, the state could do for religion was 'to let it alone—neither pamper nor persecute it'.[23]

The dignity and the final success of the Jews' struggle could not fail to influence and strengthen their status in colonial society. Not only did it gain them religious equality, but it rendered their *de facto* yet undefined civil and political equality secure and unassailable. They gained perhaps even more than that. For the campaign provided the articulate Jewish communities with the opportunity and with the platform, in the colonial legislatures and the press, to make themselves known to colonial society and to inform it of themselves and their aspirations. The Australian public was thus enabled to form an image of the colonial Jew which was very much at variance with the stereotype Old Clothes Jew of Petticoat Lane which many brought with them from the old world. How well Jews in the Australian colonies succeeded in throwing off at least part of the 'old world' prejudice against them, can be gauged from the countless reference to their 'respectability' and civic worth in the legislatures and in the press, not only by their friends but also by adversaries like James Martin in New South Wales, Pohlman and à Beckett in Victoria, or Captain Langdon in Van Diemen's Land.

The Jewish 'struggle' in the 1840s and 1850s, though a minor issue in itself, happened to be a constant and Australia-wide theme during a crucial period in Australian history. The student of history may perhaps find reflected in it some of the peculiarities and differentia in the development of the Australian communities during a period when a measure of colonial independence and responsible government was fought for and gained. The following characteristic features seem to emerge from a study of the 'struggle' in the various colonies:

In New South Wales where the movement for a measure of colonial independence and responsible government took place earliest and in its sharpest form, the Jewish agitation for a share in state aid was provoked by and directed against discriminatory instructions of the Colonial Office. Colonial opinion in the Legislative Council and in the press supported the Jewish claims against dictation by the Secretary of State. W. C. Wentworth fought for colonial independence *and* championed the Jewish cause. Victory, when it came in 1855, was more than anything the result of emancipation from the tutelage of the Colonial Office.

In Victoria the Jewish struggle was only in part and only in its earliest stage (1850–2) directed against the instructions of the Colonial Office. In its decisive phase (1853–6) it was waged by

Jews and their liberal friends against a conservative majority in the Legislative Council. In the end it was actually helped by the Colonial Office, in the person of Lord John Russell. Victorian liberals like Westgarth, Fawkner and O'Shanassy fought against conservative squatters, government officials and nominees *and* championed the Jewish cause. Thus in Victoria the Jewish victory was achieved in 1859 as part and parcel of the victory of colonial liberalism over colonial conservatism.

In Van Diemen's Land the Jewish struggle was fought against an autocratic, Tory and evangelical Lieutenant-Governor, a firm upholder of the idea of the Christian state and a believer in the religious duties of a Christian magistrate, who enjoyed the support of a conservative Secretary of State. It is therefore not surprising that Jews there had the full support of the free settlers and of their press against such an illiberal administration. When representative government and the end of transportation had been achieved, the new Legislative Council by unanimous vote, and by its representations to a more sympathetic Governor and Secretary of State, won religious equality for their Jews.

In South Australia, the 'Paradise of Dissent', one cannot even speak of a 'struggle', but rather of an attempt to put the Jewish *religion*, for there was no proper congregation yet in existence, on an equal footing with the various Christian denominations. The Jewish case was one small element in the general and powerful movement of South Australian dissenters and voluntaryists to do away with the state aid to religion which had been briefly foisted on them by a Tory Governor. Jewish equality was achieved almost a decade earlier than in the rest of the Australian colonies. Neither a Tory Governor nor Earl Grey would interfere with the unanimous wish of the local legislature to give its Jews full equality in religious and educational matters. Thus South Australia was the pioneer among Australian colonies not only in the abolition of state aid and the separation of church from state, but also in religious equality for Jews.

In all these colonies the agitation for Jewish religious equality was connected intimately with colonial liberalism, and closely with movements for the separation of church and state, and with the victory of the voluntaryist principle in religion. In South Australia in 1851 and in New South Wales in 1860–2 this connection with the voluntaryist movement was closest; in Van Diemen's Land and in Victoria, though important, the connection was less clearly defined.

Epilogue

In 1861–2, when the struggle had ended in victory, Rabbi Jacob
Saphir of Palestine visited Australia on a charitable mission for the
Jewish poor of Jerusalem. He was widely travelled and an intelligent and shrewd observer. He met the Jewish communities of
Sydney, Melbourne, Adelaide, Hobart and some provincial towns,
and he recorded his impressions in his travel book *Eben Saphir*
(*Sapphire Stone*).[1] He noted with satisfaction the prosperity and
wealth of the Australian Jews. He praised their generosity and
charity. He severely censured their laxity in matters of religious
observance, but he was most impressed with their social standing
and prestige. The Jewish merchants of Sydney, he observed, 'are
held in honour and respect by their fellow citizens', the Melbourne
Jewish community is 'highly respected in the land', and the Jews
of Adelaide 'are respectable merchants and generous people'. He
thus summed up his findings:

> In this land . . . they have learned that the Jew also possesses good
> qualities, and hatred towards him has entirely disappeared here . . .
> there is no discrimination made between nation and nation. The
> Jews live in safety, and take their share in all the good things of the
> country. They also occupy Government positions and administrative
> posts . . .[2]

Allowing some overstatement to an observer who himself came
from a situation of Jewish rightlessness and social inferiority, Rabbi
Saphir's account is a reasonable summing up of the status and
fortunes of the Australian Jewish community as a distinguishable
and by and large integrated and accepted minority group within
Australian society. That position, so it seems to me, was established
in the 1840s and 1850s when, carried on a wave of colonial liberalism and egalitarianism, Australian Jews fought for their equal rights.

1

That achievement has never been seriously challenged, not even during the critical 1930s. The reasons are perhaps not far to seek. If sceptical Australians ever had an ideology it has been the liberal democratic-egalitarian creed, a 'fair go' for all. Those who subscribe to it are not likely to nurture deeply hostile feelings against Jews, even if for one reason or another they dislike them. Moreover, Australia has so far lacked those very groups or classes which elsewhere have been notorious for their 'Jew-consciousness'. It neither inherited nor did it ever produce a large group of hard-pressed petty bourgeois who actually were, or merely felt, threatened by the success of Jewish businessmen and entrepreneurs, nor a privileged ruling class which in times of trouble would be tempted to use the Jews as a scapegoat. Nor has Australia known an 'academic proletariat' which, jealous of the material achievement and resentful of the rationalist spirit of Jewish professionals and intellectuals, would carry a message of racial hatred and Jew-baiting to struggling and bewildered shopkeepers or to a depressed and ignorant peasantry. These classes and groups, classical breeding-grounds of aggressive nationalism, violent racialism and militant antisemitism in Europe, have not yet found a place in Australian society.

Australian society, however, contained from its earliest days a large and increasingly self-conscious Irish Catholic religious-ethnic minority group. Ever since Governor Sir Richard Bourke's Church Act 'emancipated' them, Australia's Irish Catholics guarded their political and religious equality jealously and constantly challenged the English and Protestant ties of the majority. They made Australia into a pluralist society and thus facilitated the struggle for equality and integration of Australia's Jews, a smaller minority, but equally self-conscious and determined.

Thus, unlike their brethren in central and western Europe who responded with defensive timidity and self-denial to the fierce resistance their emancipation had to overcome,[3] Australia's Jews seem to have learned a better lesson—that those who crave for integration and acceptance must first accept themselves without self-delusion for what they are; only those are respected who beg neither toleration nor favour, but stand up for themselves.

Appendix

Analysis of Votes on State Aid to Jewish Religion in the Legislative Council of Victoria on 10 September 1852, 16 February and 17 March 1854*

1. W. Westgarth's motion of 10 September 1852 for 'a sum of money in aid of the community of the Jews of this colony, proportionately to similar aids presently awarded to other religious denominations of the colony.'

21 voted: 10 ayes; 11 noes.

The ten ayes consisted of:

Nine elected members:

> Charles Dight
> J. P. Fawkner
> J. S. Johnston
> Henry Miller
> John O'Shanassy
> J. T. Smith
> Peter Snodgrass
> William Westgarth
> Thomas Wilkinson

One nominee: Lieutenant-Colonel Joseph Anderson

All ten ayes voted on the land question on 28 July 1852 when W. Rutledge moved that 'leases be immediately issued to the occupants of Crown lands'; seven voted against Rutledge's 'celebrated ukase' and thus gave an anti-squatting vote, three voted in favour. Of the seven 'anti-

* Based on voting lists published in the *Argus* and in the *Votes and Proceedings* of the Legislative Council of Victoria. Divisions of elected members of Council into 'liberal' and 'squatting' members and the use of the term 'popular party' have been adopted from the *Argus*, 18, 21 February and the *Melbourne Morning Herald*, 17 February 1854.

squatters', six, namely, Fawkner, Westgarth, O'Shanassy, Miller, Johnston and Smith were both champions of the Jewish cause *and* the leading spokesmen in the Legislative Council against the squatting interest.

Of the nine who gave an anti-squatting vote on 28 July 1852, and had occasion to vote on state aid to Jews, eight voted in favour and only one (J. F. Strachan of Geelong) against.

The eleven noes consisted of:

Five officials:

> James Croke (Solicitor-General)
> C. H. Ebden (Auditor-General)
> William Lonsdale (Colonial Secretary)
> R. W. Pohlman (Chairman of Quarter Sessions)
> W. F. Stawell (Attorney-General)

Three nominees:

> T. T. à Beckett
> J. C. Riddell
> Andrew Russell

Three elected members:

> Dr Francis Murphy ⎤
> William Rutledge ⎬ leading squatters
> W. F. Splatt ⎦

Six leading squatters reported to be present at a squatters' meeting in September 1852 (reported in the *Argus*, 4 September 1852 as the 'grand meeting of the Quadrupedes') had occasion to vote on state aid to Jews. Five voted against: J. C. Riddell, William Campbell, Colin Campbell, John Goodman, W. F. Splatt. One, Dr Francis Murphy, voted in 1852 against and in 1854 in favour.

The September 1852 vote on Westgarth's motion seems to suggest that in 1852 support for the admission of Jews to state aid came chiefly from elected 'anti-squatting' members and that it was opposed by five officials, three nominees and three elected 'squatting' members.

2. On 16 February 1854 J. P. Fawkner moved for the inclusion of 'Hebrew religion' into the Public Worship clause of the new constitution.

> 31 voted: 15 ayes; 16 noes.

The fifteen ayes consisted of:

Eight elected 'liberal' members:

> George Annand
> W. B. Burnley
> J. P. Fawkner

Dr A. F. Greeves
John Hodgson
Patrick O'Brien
John O'Shanassy
George Winter

Three officials:

H. C. E. Childers (Collector of Customs)
Andrew Clarke (Surveyor-General)
James MacMahon (Chief Commissioner of Police)

The Speaker: Dr J. F. Palmer (a liberal with strong views regarding religious equality and national education)

One nominee: Andrew Russell (a banker and a friend of David Benjamin)

Two elected 'squatting' members:

Mark Nicholson ⎱ who both expressed strong views
James Thompson ⎰ regarding religious equality

The sixteen noes consisted of:

Four officials:

J. F. L. Foster (Colonial Secretary)
E. Grimes (Auditor-General)
R. W. Pohlman (Chairman of General Sessions)
W. F. Stawell (Attorney-General)

One nominee: J. C. Riddell

Five elected 'squatting' members:

William Campbell
John Goodman
C. J. Griffith
W. T. Mollison
W. F. Splatt

Six elected 'liberal' members:

John Myles ⎫
J. T. Charlton (silent vote) ⎬ extreme abolitionists
James Cowie (silent vote) ⎭
W. C. Haines (silent vote) ⎱ conservative
J. F. Strachan (silent vote) ⎰ liberals
Captain John Dane (silent vote)

3. On 17 March 1854 John O'Shanassy presented a Petition of the Jews of Melbourne against limiting state aid to Christian churches and moved that the word 'Christian' be struck out from the Public Worship clause in the new constitution.

28 voted: 12 ayes; 16 noes.

The twelve ayes consisted of:

Eight elected 'liberal' members:

> Captain G. W. Cole
> J. P. Fawkner
> John Hodgson
> William Nicholson
> Patrick O'Brien
> John O'Shanassy
> J. T. Smith
> W. C. Haines (a waverer)

Two officials:

> H. C. E. Childers (Collector of Customs)
> Andrew Clarke (Surveyor-General)

The Speaker: Dr J. F. Palmer

One elected 'squatting' member: Dr Francis Murphy

The sixteen noes consisted of:

Five officials:

> J. F. L. Foster (Colonial Secretary)
> E. Grimes (Auditor-General)
> James MacMahon (Chief Commissioner of Police)
> W. F. Stawell (Attorney-General)
> W. H. Wright (Chief Commissioner of Gold Fields)

One nominee: T. T. à Beckett (a Christian-state champion *par excellence*)

Four elected 'squatting' members:

> William Campbell
> C. J. Griffith
> W. T. Mollison
> W. F. Splatt

Six elected 'liberal' members:

> J. T. Charlton ⎫ extreme
> John Myles ⎭ abolitionists
> James Cowie
> Captain J. Dane
> George Winter (a waverer)
> J. F. Strachan (a Christian-state man)

(It is significant that with the exception of John Myles all 'liberal' elected members who voted against the extension of state aid to Jews gave a silent vote.)

4. On 17 March 1854 after O'Shanassy's move to do away with a Christian definition of the Public Worship clause had failed, J. P. Fawkner moved that the word 'Hebrew' be added to the word 'Christian'.

27 voted: 12 ayes; 15 noes.

The twelve ayes consisted of:

Seven elected 'liberal' members:

> Captain G. W. Cole
> J. P. Fawkner
> John Hodgson
> William Nicholson
> Patrick O'Brien
> John O'Shanassy
> J. T. Smith

Three officials:

> H. C. E. Childers (Collector of Customs)
> Andrew Clarke (Surveyor-General)
> J. MacMahon (Chief Commissioner of Police)

The Speaker: Dr J. F. Palmer

One elected 'squatting' member: Dr Francis Murphy

The fifteen noes consisted of:

Four officials:

> J. F. L. Foster
> E. Grimes
> W. F. Stawell
> W. H. Wright

One nominee: T. T. à Beckett

Four elected 'squatting' members:

> William Campbell
> C. J. Griffith
> W. T. Mollison
> W. F. Splatt

Six elected 'liberal' members:

> John Myles
> J. T. Charlton ⎤
> James Cowie ⎟
> Captain J. Dane ⎬ silent vote
> W. C. Haines ⎟
> J. F. Strachan ⎦

The votes of 16 February and 17 March 1854 on the question of the
extension of state aid to the Jewish religion are obviously more complex
than the vote of 10 September 1852 and that much more difficult to
interpret, especially when detailed information concerning the political
and religious opinions and affiliations of the members involved is hard
to obtain; this was particularly the case with regard to those four
'liberal' members, Cowie, Charlton, Strachan, Captain Dane, who voted
against the extension of state aid to Jews without ever taking part in
the debates.

Whatever the complexity of the February and March 1854 votes,
they appear nevertheless as of one piece with the September 1852 vote
in so far as on all occasions when a vote on the Jewish question was
taken, the active opposition to Jewish religious equality was initiated,
led and sustained by a hard core of leading conservative officials, nominees and squatters, namely:

T. T. à Beckett	W. T. Mollison
William Campbell	R. W. Pohlman
J. F. L. Foster	J. C. Riddell
John Goodman	W. F. Splatt
C. J. Griffith	W. F. Stawell
E. Grimes	W. H. Wright

These conservatives had the active support of the extreme abolitionist
John Myles, and the silent votes of two extreme abolitionists James
Cowie and J. T. Charlton, of the conservative liberal and Christian-
state man J. F. Strachan, and of Captain John Dane.

Likewise, it appears that in 1854 as in 1852, the champions of
Jewish equality belonged largely to that same anti-squatting, liberal-
radical 'popular party', namely:

George Annand	John Hodgson
W. B. Burnley	William Nicholson
Captain G. W. Cole	Patrick O'Brien
J. P. Fawkner	John O'Shanassy
Dr A. F. Greeves	J. T. Smith

These 'liberals' could command the active support of government-party
liberals like H. C. E. Childers (Collector of Customs), and J. F. Palmer
(Speaker), the silent vote of Andrew Clarke (Surveyor-General) and
the occasional support and votes of the 'squatting' members Mark
Nicholson, James Thompson and Dr Francis Murphy.

Abbreviations

A.D.B.	*Australian Dictionary of Biography* (ed. Douglas Pike)
A.J.H.S.	Australian Jewish Historical Society, *Journal and Proceedings*
C.O.	Colonial Office
C.S.O.	Chief Secretary's Office
H.R.A.	*Historical Records of Australia*, Series I
M.H.C.	Melbourne Hebrew Congregation
Parl. Deb.	*Parliamentary Debates*
P.P.	*Parliamentary Papers*
P.R.O.	Public Record Office, London
V.D.L.	Van Diemen's Land
V. & P.	*Votes and Proceedings*

Notes

1 The Age of Liberalism and Emancipation

1 For documents related to the early period of Jewish emancipation see Raphael Mahler, *Jewish Emancipation, A Selection of Documents*, pp. 25-36.
2 See Board of Deputies of British Jews, entries for 11 June 1829 and 26 April 1830, Minute Book no. 2, pp. 26, 44-5.
3 Helga Krohn, *Die Juden in Hamburg 1800-1850*, pp. 59-60.
4 Mahler, op. cit., pp. 39-40.
5 Hugo Bieber (ed.), *Heinrich Heine: Bekenntnis zum Judentum (Confessio Judaica)* (Berlin, 1925), pp. 148-57.
6 Paul Lindau (ed.), *Ferdinand Lassalle's Tagebuch* (Breslau, 1891), pp. 85-6, 160-1, entries for 2 February and 21 May 1840.
7 First published in 1860. (New York, 1918), pp. 66-7.
8 S. W. Baron, *A Social and Religious History of the Jews*, vol. 2, pp. 329-30.
9 Letter from meeting of Jews in Philadelphia, 30 August 1840, to Board of Deputies of British Jews, Minute Book no. 3, p. 48.
10 16 September 1841, editorial.
11 *Jewish Chronicle*, 15 October 1852, 3 February 1854.
12 Ibid., 15 October 1852.
13 13 March 1843, in Karl Marx and Friedrich Engels, *Werke*, vol. 27 (Berlin, 1963), p. 418.
14 'Das Judentum in der Musik' [1869] in Richard Wagner, *Gesammelte Schriften und Dichtungen*, vol. 4 (Leipzig, n.d.), p. 67.
15 Mahler, op. cit., pp. 47-52.
16 In 1854 the Jewish Disabilities Removal Act, 8 & 9 Vic., c. 52 admitted Jews to municipal offices; in 1858 the Jewish Relief Act, 21 & 22 Vic., c. 49 opened to them the House of Commons; in 1866 the Parliamentary Oaths Act, 29 & 30 Vic., c. 19 deprived the House of Lords of the right (conceded to them in 1858) to refuse admission to Jewish peers.
17 In July 1820 John Cam Hobhouse gave notice of his intention to move for the removal of Jewish disabilities 'which would be hardly believed to exist in such an age as this', but he does not seem to have followed it up. (*Parl. Deb.* (U.K.), II, vol. 2, p. 473; Cecil Roth, *A History of the Jews in England*, p. 248.)
18 *Parl. Deb.* (U.K.), II, vol. 18, p. 1592.
19 *Jewish Chronicle*, 1 June 1854; *Parl. Deb.* (U.K.), III, vol. 96, pp. 220-83.
20 *Parl. Deb.* (U.K.), III, vol. 57, p. 757. [755.
21 Ibid., p. 757.
22 Quoted in H. S. Q. Henriques, *The Jews and the English Law*, p. 287.
23 *Parl. Deb.* (U.K.), III, vol. 17, pp. 242, 1343, vol. 39, pp. 510, 516, vol. 56, p. 507; II, vol. 23, p. 1317, vol. 24, p. 793; Henriques, op. cit., pp. 268-86.

24 Thomas Babington Macaulay, *Critical and Historical Essays*, vol. 2 (Dent, London, 1907), p. 226.

25 *Parl. Deb.* (U.K.), II, vol. 23, p. 1313.

26 Henriques, op. cit., p. 290.

27 *Parl. Deb.* (U.K.), III, vol. 39, p. 515.

28 Ibid., vol. 17, p. 242.

29 Ibid., II, vol. 23, p. 1299.

30 Ibid., III, vol. 20, p. 238.

31 Ibid., vol. 17, p. 1227.

32 Morris U. Schappes, *Documentary History of Jews in the United States 1654-1875*, p. 571.

33 13 Geo. II, c. 7; Mahler, op. cit., pp. 13-15.

34 Bourke to Stanley, 30 September 1833, *H.R.A.*, vol. 17, p. 227.

35 7 Geo. IV, c. 28 and 11 Geo. IV, c. 16 (January), 1 Wm. IV, c. 57 (Lower Canada); for details and amendments see *P.P.* (1850), vol. 34, pp. 8, 13, 16-7; Mahler, op. cit., pp. 44-7.

36 *Parl. Deb.* (U.K.), II, vol. 23, p. 1291.

37 James Larra, the 'honest Jew of Parramatta' became sergeant-major of the Loyal Parramatta Association in 1804; G. F. J. Bergman, 'James Larra, the commercial nabob of Parramatta', *A.J.H.S.*, vol. 5, pp. 108-9.

38 Alfred Stephen to Deas Thomson, 25 November 1844, *H.R.A.*, vol. 24, p. 388; also statement of former Attorney-General, J. H. Plunkett, in the Legislative Assembly of New South Wales on 19 August 1856, *Sydney Morning Herald*, 20 August 1856.

39 *Empire*, 24 October 1854.

40 7 Wm. IV, no. 3—an Act to promote the building of churches and chapels and to provide for the maintenance of ministers of religion in New South Wales.

41 5 & 6 Vic., c. 76.

42 In South Australia where state aid to religion was introduced in 1846, Jews were conceded a proportionate share in the same year. In Queensland and Western Australia the question of state aid to Jewish religion (as distinct from state grants of land for synagogues) appar-

ently never arose. In Queensland (which separated from New South Wales in 1859) the Legislative Council abolished state aid to religion during its first session in 1860. (See Charles Arrowsmith Bernays, *Queensland Politics during Sixty (1859-1919) Years* (Brisbane, 1919), p. 19.) In Western Australia where Jewish congregational institutions began to function in the early 1890s, state aid to religion was abolished in 1895, i.e. before Jews who had no rabbi then (the first arrived in 1897) would have been eligible to claim state aid. (See David J. Benjamin, 'Western Australian Jewry', *A.J.H.S.*, vol. 2, pp. 261, 294-8, 305, 372, 378.)

43 *Sydney Morning Herald*, 21 September 1844; *Voice of Jacob*, 25 April 1845.

44 19 October 1846, Sydney Synagogue Letter Book 19 October 1846–27 September 1859, p. 1.

45 *Jewish Chronicle*, 20 May 1847.

2 New South Wales 1788-1844

1 'A Magistrate', *A Treatise on the Police of the Metropolis.*

2 This estimate is based on communications to me of Dr G. F. J. Bergman (Sydney) and Rabbi John Levi (Melbourne) who work on the identification of Jewish convicts.

3 See New South Wales Census, November 1828, P.R.O. London, H.O. 10/21, where the entries usually indicate the religion and status (free or bond) of the person listed.

4 Ralph Mansfield, *Analytical View of the Census of New South Wales 1841*, pp. 21, 46. Using the Indents of Convict Ships 1790 to 1835, the Muster of New South Wales of 1814 and the Census of New South Wales of 1828, I have found some 134 fully identified Jewish convicts, some 33 who were most probably Jewish and 91 who in all probability were Jewish. Allowing for those who could not be identi-

fied as Jews because they left or died before 1828 or did not declare themselves as Jews in 1828, I have arrived at an estimate of over three hundred convicts; this tallies with Dr Bergman's estimate, based on his study of shipping lists 1829-1836, of some 150 free Jewish settlers to have arrived in New South Wales until 1836.

5 See the analysis of the places of birth and of conviction of Jewish convicts in Israel Getzler, 'Neither toleration nor favour: The struggle of the Jewish communities in the Australian colonies for equal religious rights in the 1840s and 1850s' (unpubl. M.A. thesis, University of Melbourne, 1960), Appendix I.

6 Cecil Roth, *A History of the Jews in England*, pp. 232-4; 'The Jews of western Europe' in Louis Finkelstein (ed.), *The Jews: Their history, culture and religion*, vol. 1, pp. 258-9.

7 A. M. Hyamson, *A History of the Jews in England*, pp. 236-8.

8 V. D. Lipman, *Social History of the Jews in England 1850-1950*, p. 6.

9 Ibid.

10 Op. cit., pp. 40, 159; Joshua van Oven to Patrick Colquhoun, 24 March 1801 in Cecil Roth (ed.), *Anglo-Jewish Letters 1158-1917* (London, 1938), pp. 210-19.

11 Colquhoun, op. cit., pp. 49, 51-2, 113, 119-20, 158-9, 176.

12 Getzler, op. cit., Appendix I.

13 [Colquhoun], op. cit., pp. 158, 176; Henry Fielding, *An Enquiry into the Causes of the late Increase of Robbers* in *The Works of Henry Fielding*, 3rd ed., vol. 11 (London, 1766), pp. 335-41.

14 Quoted in M. Clark, 'The origins of the convicts transported to eastern Australia, 1787-1852', *Historical Studies, Australia and New Zealand*, no. 26 (May 1956), p. 134.

15 *Report of the Committee of the Sydney Synagogue 1845*, p. 7.

16 Lipman, op. cit., pp. 41-44.

17 *Historical Records of New South Wales*, vol. 2, p. 759.

18 *A.D.B.* vol. 2, p. 109; New South Wales Census, November 1828, nos 711-14.

19 New South Wales Census, November 1828, nos 7-10, 956-7, 1062, 1720-3, 4012, 1998.

20 *H.R.A.*, vol. 9, p. 373.

21 The relevant records of the Board of Deputies of British Jews, Minute Book no. 1, November 1760 to April 1828, contain no reference whatever to Jews in New South Wales or Van Diemen's Land.

22 See Indents of Convict Ships 1818-19.

23 G. F. J. Bergman, 'Edward Davis: Life and death of an Australian bushranger', *A.J.H.S.*, vol. 4, pp. 205-40.

24 *Report*, p. 7.

25 I owe this information to the kindness of Dr G. F. J. Bergman who made his extracts of shipping lists 1829-36 available to me.

26 For J. B. Montefiore, see *A.D.B.*, vol. 2 pp. 250-1; for P. J. Cohen, see *A.J.H.S.*, vol. 3, pp. 370-1; vol. 4, pp. 84-5.

27 *H.R.A.*, vol. 14, pp. 243-5.

28 Ibid., vol. 14, pp. 2, 618; vol. 15, pp. 77, 308.

29 Ibid., vol. 14, p. 618.

30 *Report*, p. 7.

31 Ibid.

32 *Report of the Sydney Synagogue 1845*, p. 7.

33 Ibid.; also Cecil Roth, 'Rabbi Aaron Levy's mission to Australia', *A.J.H.S.*, vol. 3, pp. 1-6.

34 *Laws and Rules for the Management and Regulation of the Sydney Synagogue* (Sydney, 1833).

35 Ibid.; *Report*, p. 8.

36 Ralph Mansfield, *Analytical View of the Census of New South Wales for the Year 1846*, pp. 21, 46.

37 This statement is based on information contained in the 1828 Census, in the New South Wales Almanacks for 1834 and 1835, in a list of Jewish electors to the Sydney city elections of 1842, *A.J.H.S.*, vol. 1, pp. 275-7. In May 1842 George Moss in the first number of the Sydney *Voice of Jacob*, p. 3, stated that 'a very large proportion of the Hebrew body in New South Wales is concerned in trade'.

38 7 Wm. IV, no. 3, 'An Act to promote the building of churches and
chapels and to provide for the
maintenance of ministers of religion in New South Wales.'

39 Bourke to Stanley, 30 September
1833, *H.R.A.*, vol. 17, pp. 224-30.

40 Ibid. p. 229.

41 Quoted in John Barrett, *That Better
Country: The religious aspect of
life in eastern Australia* (Melbourne, 1966), p. 35.

42 Major William Bolden Dundas
appearing before a Select Committee of the House of Commons on
6 August 1835 commented thus
on Bourke's famous 50th Ordinance of 1828: 'General Bourke's
ordinance emancipated (I think
you may say so) the Hottentots
altogether'. See *P.P.* (1835), vol.
39, part 2, pp. 5-33; *P.P.* (1836),
vol. 7, reports.

43 See the Sir Richard Bourke Papers,
vol. 9 (Mitchell Library, Sydney)
for Bourke's correspondence with
Thomas Spring-Rice (later Lord
Monteagle) from 10 September
1823 to 9 May 1855 and for the
letters of condolence which Lord
Monteagle received upon the death
of his friend Bourke on 12 August
1855.

44 *A.D.B.*, vol. 2, p. 338.

45 Michael Roe, *The Quest for Authority in Eastern Australia 1835-
1851* (Melbourne, 1965), p. 110.

46 The English Church Building Acts
before 1836 do not contain anything like this preamble. See 58
Geo. III, c. 45; 3 Geo. IV, c. 72;
5 Geo. IV, c. 103; 7 & 8 Geo. IV,
c. 72; 1 & 2 Wm. IV, c. 38; 2 & 3
Wm. IV, c. 61. The Canadian
Clergy Endowments Acts of 1774,
14 Geo. III, c. 83 and the Repeal
Act of 1791, 31 Geo. III, c. 31 and
c. 35 refer to the 'Protestant Religion' and the 'Religion of the
Church of Rome' specifically and
not to 'Christian' religion or 'Christian' worship undefined. In fact
both Governor Bourke and the
Secretary of State, Glenelg, were
aware that Bourke's religious
scheme was an innovation. (See
H.R.A., vol. 18, p. 203.)

47 Broughton to Glenelg, 3 December
1835, *H.R.A.*, vol. 18, p. 700.

48 Bourke to Glenelg, 14 September
1836, *H.R.A.*, vol. 18, p. 537.

49 A. Cohen, 'President of the Israel-
itish community', to Sir Richard
Bourke, November, 1837, *A.J.H.S.*,
vol. 1, p. 144.

50 H. F. Gisbourne (Bourke's private
secretary) to A. Cohen, 4 December 1837, ibid., pp. 144-5.

51 Ralph Mansfield, *Analytical View
of the Census . . . 1846*, p. 81.

52 *V. & P.* (L.C.N.S.W.) (1832-7),
pp. 195-6.

53 Brian Fitzpatrick, *British Imperialism and Australia*, pp. 309-10, 372.

54 *Australian Almanack and Directory*
(Sydney, 1835), p. 339.

55 See, e.g., A. L. Benjamin, 'Jewish
colonists in Melbourne's early land
sales', *A.J.H.S.*, vol. 2, pp. 223-6.

56 Jacob Levi Montefiore (Sydney)
to S. Cohen (London), 6 November 1846 (private letter, Mitchell
Library, Sydney).

57 *A.J.H.S.*, vol. 1, p. 23.

58 Ibid., vol. 2, p. 65.

59 The Jewish Philanthropic Society
supported some twenty destitute
Jews with weekly allowances; see
Sydney Synagogue Minute Book,
1837-47, pp. 49-50, for correspondence between Deas Thomson,
Isaac Simmons and Captain Alex-
ander Maconochie regarding the
religious needs of nine Jewish convicts in Norfolk Island.

60 Sydney Synagogue Minute Book,
1837-47, p. 126.

61 *Voice of Jacob*, 28 August 1846.

62 In 1843 the *Voice of Jacob* listed
Lewis Barnet, Samuel Benjamin,
Ambrose Elias, Elias Ellis, Israel
Joseph, Abraham Moses, Solomon
Phillips and Emanuel Phillips as
subscribers in Sydney.

63 *Voice of Jacob*, 25 November 1842.

64 See D. J. Benjamin, 'The Sydney
Voice of Jacob', *A.J.H.S.*, vol. 2,
pp. 443-68, for all the Australian
materials published in the three
issues of the Sydney *Voice of
Jacob*, 27 May, 24 June, 15 September 1842; also P. J. Marks,
'The Jewish Press of Australia',
A.J.H.S., vol. 1, pp. 302-15.

65 *Voice of Jacob* (Sydney), 15 September, 27 May 1842.

66 Sydney Synagogue Minutes 1837-47, entry for 1 March 1840.

67 For the Robert Lowe Report 1844, see D. C. Griffiths (ed.), *Documents in the Establishment of Education in New South Wales 1789-1880* (Melbourne, 1957), pp. 74-5.

68 Ibid.

69 The following account of the meeting is based on the extensive reports published in the *Sydney Morning Herald*, 21 September 1844 and the *Voice of Jacob*, 25 April 1845.

70 *Voice of Jacob*, 25 April 1845.

71 18, 19 September 1844.

72 *Sydney Morning Herald*, 3 October 1844.

73 Ibid.

74 Ibid., 28 November, 20 December 1844.

75 *Report of the Sydney Synagogue 1845*, p. 9.

76 *Sydney Morning Herald*, 21 September 1844.

77 *Voice of Jacob*, 25 April 1845.

3 *New South Wales 1845-1846*

1 *Report*, p. 9.

2 Ibid., p. 17.

3 *Australian*, 19 September, 2 October 1844; *Examiner*, 4, 11 October 1845.

4 Sydney Synagogue Minute Book, 1837-47, p. 158.

5 *V. & P.* (L.C.N.S.W.) (1845), p. 185.

6 *Sydney Morning Herald*, 25 October 1845.

7 He seems to allude here to the Maynooth College Endowment Bill of April 1845.

8 It was very likely on Plunkett's advice that in 1842 the Church Act was not repealed by the Constitution Act; see Plunkett to Stanley, 8 October 1842, Stanley to Gipps, 24 August 1844, *H.R.A.*, vol. 23, pp. 734-5; Plunkett, as a staunch Catholic, had good reason to see the Church Act, the Australian

version of Catholic emancipation, preserved.

9 *A.D.B.*, vol. 3, p. 476.

10 *Sydney Morning Herald*, 25 October 1845.

11 *Cumberland Times*, 1 November 1845; *Examiner*, 25 October 1845.

12 1 November 1845.

13 26 November 1845.

14 See *Sydney Morning Herald*, 27, 29 November, 9, 12, 23, 26 December 1845; *Atlas*, 13 December 1845.

15 *Sydney Morning Herald*, 26 November 1845.

16 Ibid., 29 November 1845.

17 13 December 1845, signed O.L.

18 25 October 1845.

19 *Sydney Morning Herald*, 25 October 1845.

20 Stanley to Gipps, 24 August 1844, *H.R.A.*, vol. 23, pp. 732-8; Gipps to Stanley, 7 August 1845, ibid., vol. 24, pp. 440-3.

21 See Gipps to Stanley, 28 March 1846, ibid., vol. 24, p. 829.

22 Gipps to Stanley, 21 January 1844, ibid., vol. 23, p. 350.

23 Gipps to Stanley, 13 November 1845, ibid., vol. 24, p. 612.

24 See pp. 62-3.

25 C.O. 201/358, minute of 8 May 1846.

26 Ibid., minute of 9 May 1846.

27 Gladstone to Gipps, 17 January 1846, *H.R.A.*, vol. 24, pp. 712-15.

28 W. E. Gladstone, *The State in its Relations with the Church*, *passim*; *Church Principles considered in their Results*, p. 370.

29 Gladstone to FitzRoy, 4 June 1846, *H.R.A.*, vol. 25, p. 83.

30 11 November 1845.

31 *Sydney Morning Herald*, 3 June 1846; *V. & P.* (L.C.N.S.W.) (1st Session, 1846), p. 33.

32 *Sydney Morning Herald*, 16 September 1846.

33 Ibid.

34 *A.D.B.*, vol. 1, p. 385.

35 *V. & P.* (L.C.N.S.W.) (2nd session, 1846), p. 209.

36 FitzRoy to Gladstone, 1 October 1846, *H.R.A.*, vol. 25, p. 202.

37 'Letter to Deputies, London', 19 October 1846, in Sydney Synagogue Letter Book, October 1846-

September 1859. Also ibid., 'Letter from Moses Montefiore', 26 August 1847.

38 *Voice of Jacob*, 20 May 1847; also see Jacob Levi Montefiore to S. Cohen, 6 November 1846, private letter (Mitchell Library, Sydney).

39 C.O. 201/369.

40 Report on Jamaica Act no. 1840, 25 January 1828, C.O. 323/45, folios 98-103; also see Paul Knaplund, *James Stephen and the Colonial Office 1813-1847*, pp. 149-50 for Stephen's approval of the Lower Canada Bill, no. 683 of 1830, which improved the political position of Jews.

41 Knaplund, op. cit., p. 19.

42 Ibid., p. 158.

43 C.O. 201/369, minute of 22 March 1847.

44 S. Maccoby, *English Radicalism 1832-1852* (London, 1935), pp. 72-3, 163, 266.

45 *Parl. Deb.* (U.K.), III, vol. 56, p. 507, vol. 39, p. 518, vol. 82, p. 643.

46 *Parl. Deb.* (U.K.), III, vol. 149, p. 14; Hyamson, op. cit., p. 265.

47 C.O. 201/369.

48 Grey to FitzRoy, 13 April 1847, *H.R.A.*, vol. 25, pp. 484-6.

49 'Report . . . for the Year 5607', *A.J.H.S.*, vol. 5, p. 77.

4   *New South Wales 1849-1855*

1 *Sydney Morning Herald*, 29 August 1849.

2 See K. N. Bell and W. P. Morrell, *Select Documents on British Colonial Policy* (Oxford, 1928), pp. 57-8.

3 *Sydney Morning Herald*, 29 August 1849.

4 *Parl. Deb.* (U.K.), III, vol. 95, pp. 1322-30.

5 *V. & P.* (L.C.N.S.W.), vol. 1 1949), 28 August 1849, p. 207.

6 See p. 86.

7 Grey to FitzRoy, 26 May 1851, C.O. 201/432.

8 Israel Porush, 'Rev. Herman Hoelzel—The first qualified Jewish Minister in Australia', *A.J.H.S.*, vol. 2, p. 181.

9 *V. & P.* (L.C.N.S.W.), vol. 1 (1853), 16 August 1853, p. 159.

10 *Sydney Morning Herald*, 21 September 1853.

11 *Jewish Chronicle*, 27 January 1854.

12 *Sydney Morning Herald*, 21 September 1853; *Empire*, 22 September 1853.

13 21 September 1853.

14 *Sydney Morning Herald*, 23 August 1854.

15 *Empire*, 23 August 1854; regarding the original draft of Bourke's Church Act, see Israel Getzler, 'Neither toleration nor favour', unpubl. M.A. thesis, University of Melbourne, 1960.

16 Martin seems to refer to Lord Aberdeen's Bill of 29 April 1853.

17 *Sydney Morning Herald*, 23 August 1854. It is worth noting that in 1867 James Martin gave his opinion as Attorney-General that 'it is not obligatory on the Council [of Education of New South Wales] to certify a school belonging to [the Jewish] persuasion', David J. Benjamin, 'The Sydney Hebrew Certified Denomination School', *A.J.H.S.*, vol. 4, pp. 243-4.

18 *Sydney Morning Herald*, 23 August 1854.

19 *V. & P.* (L.C.N.S.W.), vol. 1 (1854), 21 September 1854, p. [170.

20 Ibid., 3 October 1854.

21 FitzRoy to Grey, 18 October 1854, C.O. 201/476.

22 C.O. 201/476, minute of 29 January 1855.

23 H. Merivale, *Lectures on Colonization and Colonies, Delivered before the University of Oxford in 1839, 1840 and 1841*, p. 602.

24 *Dictionary of National Biography*, vol. 13, p. 281.

25 C.O. 201/476, minute of 8 May 1855; also see A. C. V. Melbourne, *Early Constitutional Development in Australia: New South Wales 1788-1856*, p. 425.

26 Russell to FitzRoy, 21 May 1855, C.O. 201/476; the section italicized by me was added to the draft by Russell in his own handwriting.

27 *V. & P.* (L.C.N.S.W.), vol. 1

(1855), 21 September 1855, p. 911.

28 Entry for 6 September 1855, in Sydney Synagogue Letter Book, October 1846–September 1859.

29 Entry for 30 September 1855, ibid.

30 Ibid., pp. 95-6.

31 *Empire*, 24 October 1854.

32 *Sydney Morning Herald*, 20 August 1856; Alfred Stephen, Chief Justice of New South Wales acted thus for many years past when Jews and Quakers were required to take the oath of Abjuration, e.g. for the purpose of naturalization, see Alfred Stephen to Deas Thomson, 25 November 1844, *H.R.A.*, vol. 24, p. 389.

33 *Sydney Morning Herald*, 12 November 1856.

34 20 Vic., no. 9.

35 For reports of the meeting see *Sydney Morning Herald*, 9 November 1858; *A.J.H.S.*, vol. 1, pp. 6-18.

36 Alfred de Lissa to M. Handell, 27 January 1859 in Sydney Synagogue Letter Book 1846-59.

37 R. Flanagan, *History of New South Wales*, vol. 2, p. 377.

38 Ibid., pp. 442-3.

39 York Street Synagogue Minute Book, 1858-60.

40 *V. & P.* (L.A.N.S.W.) (1858-9), vol. 1, p. 761.

41 S. B. Glass and I. Porush, 'The Reasons for the Macquarie Street Secession', *A.J.H.S.*, vol. 3, pp. 5-28.

42 *V. & P.* (L.A.N.S.W.) (1859-60), vol. 1, p. 689; *Sydney Morning Herald*, 23 May 1860.

43 *Sydney Morning Herald*, 26 May 1860.

44 Ibid.

45 Ibid., 23 May 1860.

5 Van Diemen's Land under Franklin

1 Barnard Walford to Arthur, 21 May 1828 in Chief Secretary's Archives, Hobart, C.S.O. 269, pp. 166-8. See also W. D. Forsyth, *Governor Arthur's Convict System:* *Van Diemen's Land 1824-1836* (London, 1935), p. 39.

2 Henry Davis to Arthur, 17 September 1832, C.S.O. 613; for Arthur's reply see minute dated 19 September 1832.

3 R. M. Hartwell, *The Economic Development of Van Diemen's Land 1820-1850* (Melbourne, 1956), pp. 44-6, 73.

4 *Elliston's Hobart Town Almanack and Van Diemen's Land Annual 1837-1938* (Hobart, 1838).

5 H. I. Wolff, 'A Century of Hobart Jewry', *A.J.H.S.*, vol. 2, p. 5.

6 Quoted in *A.J.H.S.*, vol. 5, p. 341.

7 Wolff, op. cit., p. 5.

8 For Phineas Moss see G. F. J. Bergman, 'Phineas Moss (1795-1866)', *A.J.H.S.*, vol. 6, pp. 267-78; see also *Hobart Courier*, 27 May 1842, for Phineas Moss's lecture on 'Pneumatics' at the Mechanics' Institute, Hobart.

9 *Hobart Town Advertiser*, 20 September 1842.

10 Kathleen Fitzpatrick, *Sir John Franklin in Tasmania 1837-1843*, pp. 60, 110.

11 *Hobart Town Advertiser*, 20 September 1842.

12 *Voice of Jacob*, 19 January 1844.

13 For examples see *Murray's Review*, 24 March, 18 August 1843; *Colonial Times*, 15 August 1843.

14 *Statistical Account of Van Diemen's Land or Tasmania*, vol. 1, 1804-48 (Government Printer, Hobart, 1856).

15 Circular of Launceston Hebrew Congregation to 'Members of the Jewish Persuasion in Australia', September 1850.

16 Hartwell, op. cit., pp. 226-7.

17 See subscription lists in *Hobart Town Advertiser*, 13 June, 8 September 1843.

18 Hobart Hebrew Congregation Minute Book no. 1, entry for 1 May 1843.

19 J. E. Bicheno (Colonial Secretary) to Louis Nathan (President of Hobart Hebrew Congregation), 30 May 1843, C.S.O. 8/165.

20 See enclosure in Franklin to Stanley, 14 June 1843, in V.D.L. Duplicate Despatches.

21 1 Vic., no. 16, 1837, 'Support for certain Christian ministers and erection of places of divine worship.'

22 John West, *The History of Tasmania*, vol. 1, pp. 206-7.

23 Lord Stanley to Franklin, 5 September, 1842 in C. M. H. Clark, *Select Documents in Australian History 1788-1850*, p. 345.

24 W. L. Cohen, 'The inauguration of the Launceston Hebrew Congregation', *A.J.H.S.*, vol. 2, p. 413.

25 Memorial of Members of the Jewish persuasion residing in Launceston to His Excellency Sir John Franklin, C.S.O. 8/169.

26 *Cornwall Chronicle*, 4, 11 March 1843; *Launceston Examiner*, 8 March 1843.

27 11 March 1843.

28 8 March 1843.

29 For the text of the Petition, see *Launceston Examiner*, 24 May 1843; *Murray's Review*, 2 June 1843.

30 B. Francis, Moses Moss and D. Benjamin to Eardley-Wilmot, 27 November 1843, V.D.L. Duplicate Despatches.

31 *Voice of Jacob*, 24 November 1843.

32 27 May 1843.

33 31 May 1843.

34 2 June 1843.

35 Quoted in *Murray's Review*, 2 June 1843.

36 Fitzpatrick, op. cit., pp. 35, 38, 136; West, op. cit., p. 228.

37 Thomas Arnold to Franklin, 20 July 1836 in A. P. Stanley, *Life and Correspondence of Thomas Arnold*, p. 386, also pp. 372, 302, 375.

38 Fitzpatrick, op. cit., p. 184.

39 Franklin to Stanley, 14 June 1843, V.D.L. Duplicate Despatches.

40 Ibid.

41 Fitzpatrick, op. cit., p. 34.

42 Ibid., pp. 335-9, 343-4.

43 27 May 1843.

44 Moses Montefiore to Stanley, 16 November 1843, enclosure with despatch from Stanley to Eardley-Wilmot, 27 November 1843, V.D.L. Duplicate Despatches.

45 C.O., 280/157.

46 C.O. 209/20, 1702 New Zealand.

47 Stephen to Stanley, 16 October 1843, C.O. 280/157.

48 C.O. 280/157 minute dated 20 October 1843.

49 Ibid., minute dated 30 October 1843; for the Australian Land Sales Act, 1842, 5 & 6 Vic., c. 36, see K. N. Bell and W. P. Morrell, *Select Documents on British Colonial Policy* (Oxford, 1928), p. 222.

50 James Picciotto, *Sketches of Anglo-Jewish History*, p. 398.

51 See *Parl. Deb.* (U.K.), III, vol. 149, p. 1480.

52 Stanley to FitzRoy, 9 November 1843, C.O. 209/20.

53 C.O. 208/157.

54 Ibid., minute dated 16 December 1843.

55 *Parl. Deb.* (U.K.) III, vol. 39, p. 519.

56 Eardley-Wilmot to Stanley, 9 May 1844, V.D.L. Duplicate Despatches.

57 See subscription lists in *Hobart Town Advertiser*, 13 June, 8 September 1843; Circular of Launceston Hebrew Congregation, September 1850.

58 *Launceston Examiner*, 2 October 1844; *Voice of Jacob*, 28 February 1845, reprinted in David J. Benjamin, 'Australia and the *Voice of Jacob*', *A.J.H.S.*, vol. 2, pp. 300-1.

6   *Van Diemen's Land 1852-1855*

1 *Voice of Jacob*, 20 December 1844.

2 13 & 14 Vic., c. 59.

3 Hobart Hebrew Congregation Minute Book no. 1, entry for 25 April 1848.

4 Ibid., entry for 11 April 1848.

5 Ibid., entry for 27 November 1849 records receipt of letter from N. Adler, the Chief Rabbi who replied that 'passholders may form a portion of the number to constitute a *Minyan* [religious quorum] but that they are not to have any privileges conferred on them in the Synagogue'.

6 13 & 14 Vic., c. 59, clause 17.

7 W. A. Townsley, *The Struggle for Self-government in Tasmania 1842-1856*, p. 106.

[8] *V. & P.* (L.C.V.D.L.), vol. 1 (1852), p. 8.

[9] C.S.O. Letter-book of the Lieutenant-Governor and Private Secretary 1851-5, p. 22.

[10] See *A.J.H.S.*, vol. 2, pp. 108-10.

[11] Denison to Grey, 15 September 1851, Duplicate Despatches of V.D.L.

[12] W. Denison, *Varieties of Vice-regal Life*, vol. 1, pp. 173, 233.

[13] 1 Vic., no. 16; 2 Vic., no. 17; 4 Vic., no. 16; 5 Vic., no. 9; 13 Vic., no. 1.

[14] *V. & P.* (L.C.V.D.L.), vol. 3 (1853), p. 22.

[15] *Colonial Times*, 27 July 1853.

[16] Ibid., 21 July 1853.

[17] Ibid., 28 July 1853.

[18] *V. & P.* (L.C.V.D.L.), vol. 3, (1853).

[19] Ibid., papers nos 44, 51.

[20] Ibid., p. 22.

[21] *Colonial Times*, 21, 28 July 1853.

[22] *V. & P.* (L.C.V.D.L.), vol. 3 (1853), p. 136; *Colonial Times*, 17 September 1853.

[23] The American Bill of Rights of 1791 removed religion from the jurisdiction of the state when it declared: 'Congress shall make no law respecting an establishment of religion or prohibiting the free exercise of it.' In France, the state was responsible for the payment of all clergy from 1831 until the separation of church and state in 1906.

[24] While 'certain ministers' in the preamble to the Franklin Church Act referred specifically to the Churches of England, Scotland and Rome, in practice 'for many years past', the Wesleyans and Baptists received state aid.

[25] See D. Fenton, *History of Tasmania*, p. 255; *Colonial Times*, 20 September 1854.

[26] *V. & P.* (L.C.V.D.L.), vol. 4 (1854), p. 207. The original Petition is in the Mitchell Library, Sydney.

[27] *Colonial Times*, 31 October 1854.

[28] *V. & P.* (L.C.V.D.L.), vol. 4 (1854), p. 226.

[29] Though the voluntaryists J. W. Gleadow and T. G. Gregson were 'in principle opposed to any grant being made to religion' they would not call for a division, see *Colonial Times*, 31 October, 1854.

[30] *Hobart Town Advertiser*, 7 November 1854; *V. & P.* (L.C.V.D.L.), vol. 4 (1854), p. 233.

[31] T. D. Chapman to Grey, 14 November 1854, enclosure with despatch from Denison to Grey, 23 November 1854, V.D.L. Duplicate Despatches.

[32] Ibid.

[33] Phineas Moss to Louis Nathan, 16 November 1854, in letter-bundle, Hobart Synagogue.

[34] Moses Montefiore to Phineas Moss, 28 March 1855, in letter-bundle, Hobart Synagogue.

[35] John Russell to Young, 21 May 1855, V.D.L. Duplicate Despatches.

[36] *V. & P.* (L.C.V.D.L.), vol. 5 (1855), p. 164.

[37] See *Colonial Times*, 8 September 1855, for a report of the debate.

[38] Ibid.

[39] Phineas Moss to Isaac Foligno, 9 September 1855, in letter-bundle, Hobart Synagogue; '*status*' is underlined in the original draft of the letter and in the copy in the minutes of the Board of Deputies of British Jews.

[40] They received £150 annually from 1856 until 1862; £62 annually from 1862 until 1869 and a final payment of £429 in debentures as compensation for the abolition of state aid.

[41] Phineas Moss to T. D. Chapman, 8 November 1855, in letter-bundle, Hobart Synagogue.

[42] *Colonial Times*, 7 September 1855.

7 South Australia 1846-1851

[1] Douglas Pike, *Paradise of Dissent: South Australia 1829-1857*, ch. 4, especially pp. 88-9.

[2] *Morning Chronicle*, 1 July 1834 quoted in A. Fabian, 'Early days of South Australian Jewry', *A.J.H.S.*, vol. 2, p. 128.

[3] Pike, op. cit., p. 97.

[4] In 1836 Spring-Rice succeeded Robert Grant as champion of Jewish emancipation and moved for the

abolition of Jewish disabilities in the House of Commons. (See *Parl. Deb.* (U.K.), III, vol. 33, pp. 1127-37; J. Picciotto, *Sketches of Anglo-Jewish History*, pp. 390-1).

5 L. Loewe (ed.), *The Diaries of Sir Moses and Lady Montefiore*, vol. 1, p. 94, entry dated 7 May 1835.

6 Pike, op. cit., p. 115.

7 See *South Australian Almanack*, 1841, 1844, 1846 where the occupations of some early Jewish settlers are given as landholders, merchants, storekeepers, importers, clothiers and innkeepers. See also H. Munz, *Jews in South Australia 1836-1936*, pp. 18, 40, 43.

8 *South Australian News* (London), 15 March 1844.

9 The *South Australian Almanack* (Adelaide, 1843), p. 118, gives the number of Jews in the colony as ten who 'meet in Currie-street', the house of the merchant Burnett Nathan, but have 'no Synagogue'.

10 See E. L. Montefiore to Major T. S. O'Halloran, Private Secretary to the Governor, 9 August, 20 September 1843, South Australian Archives, nos 199, 266; also Philip Levi to Grey, 10 October 1843, ibid., no. 478.

11 See W. Bartley to Robert Gouger, 6 September 1843, ibid., no. 199.

12 Pike, op. cit., p. 274; *South Australian Almanack*, 1844, 1846.

13 Pike, op. cit., p. 358.

14 Robe to Gladstone, 7 December 1846, C.O. 13/50.

15 *South Australian Register*, 27 June 1846.

16 Ibid., 18 July 1846.

17 Ibid., 4 July 1846.

18 *South Australian*, 22 August 1846; *South Australian Register*, 5 August 1846.

19 *South Australian*, 22 August 1846.

20 Ibid. Under Governor Robe's State Aid Bill state aid to religion was offered at the rate of two shillings per head per annum with denominations sharing according to the religious returns in the 1846 Census. Since Morphett's motion was for six months' aid, the share of

the fifty-eight Jews who were in the colony was £2 18.

21 *South Australian Register*, 22 August 1846.

22 Ibid.

23 Ibid., 26 August 1846; also 19 September 1846.

24 Adelaide Hebrew Congregation, Minute Book no. 1, entry for 10 September 1848.

25 See *Voice of Jacob*, 28 August 1846.

26 *South Australian Register*, 2 September 1846.

27 Robe to Grey, 15 September 1846, C.O. 13/50.

28 C.O. 13/50.

29 *South Australian Almanack*, 1846, p. 138.

30 Pike, op. cit., p. 371.

31 *South Australian Register*, 17 July 1847.

32 Ibid., 24 July 1847.

33 Ibid.

34 Ibid.

35 Pike, op. cit., p. 371.

36 *South Australian*, 6 August 1847.

37 Ibid.

38 The Jewish Petition is dated 10 August 1847 and its full text was published in the *Mining Journal*, 27 February 1851.

39 Ibid.

40 *South Australian Register*, 18 August 1847.

41 South Australian Archives, nos 989, 1021, 1033, 1246, 1259, 1291.

42 Ibid., no. 1291.

43 Adelaide Hebrew Congregation, Minute Book no. 1, pp. 16, 19.

44 18 July 1849.

45 Adelaide Hebrew Congregation, Minute Book no. 1, entry for 30 June 1850; see also *Mining Journal*, 27 February 1851.

46 13 & 14 Vic.

47 Pike, op. cit., pp. 442, 432-3.

48 *South Australian Register*, 30 August 1851.

49 Ibid.

50 Adelaide Hebrew Congregation, Minute Book no. 1, entry for 27 August 1851.

51 *South Australian Register*, 30 August 1851.

52 Ibid.

53 Ibid., 19 December 1851.

54 South Australian Archives, nos 2787-8.

55 J. B. Montefiore to Charles Sturt, 19 December 1851, South Australian Archives, no. 3809.

56 John Lazar held office from 1855 to 1858. See Thomas Worsnop, *History of the City of Adelaide* (Adelaide, 1878) pp. 445-6.

57 Morris Marks 'was sworn according to the Judaic form'; *Parl. Deb.* (H. of A. S.A.) (1857-8), p. 10. The *South Australian Register*, 23 April 1857 reports that 'when the member of the Burra was called up, the Chief Secretary neglected to make the necessary distinction between the oath as administered to a Christian and a Jew; but Mr. Marks deliberately opened the Bible at the Books of Moses, and having placed his hat upon his head, took the oath according to the Judaic form.'

8 *Victoria 1850-1855*

1 L. M. Goldman, 'The early Jewish settlers in Victoria and their problems', pt 1, *A.J.H.S.*, vol. 4, pp. 336-7.

2 According to its Minutes of Proceedings, 12 September 1841 to 8 October 1843, a Jewish Congregational Society was founded on 12 September 1841 to succeed the 'Society for the Relief of Poor and Infirm Jews' which had been in existence since 1839. The Jewish Congregational Society was on 21 January 1844 given the name 'Holy Congregation of the Remnant of Israel'.

3 Minutes of Proceedings, entries for 23 April and 28 May, 1843. The grant consisted of '1 Acre adjoining the General Cemetery in Melbourne'.

4 Quoted in *A.J.H.S.* vol. 4, p. 361.

5 Minutes of Proceedings, entry for 3 September 1843.

6 Jewish Congregational Society Minute Book no. 1, entry for 14 April 1844.

7 Victorian Register of Grants, no. 80, pp. 364-7.

8 See occupations listed in the Register of Births of the Jewish Congregation for 1851.

9 See correspondence in Letter Book of the Jewish Congregation of Melbourne, Port Phillip, from 29 December 1847 to 16 July 1850.

10 A. H. Hart to H. Moore, ibid., 12 July 1850; for H. Moore's 'Church Temporalities Bill', see *Argus*, 12, 23, 25, 27 July, 1 August 1850.

11 *Argus*, 11 July 1850.

12 *Sydney Morning Herald*, 31 July, 3 August 1850.

13 Ibid., 10 August 1850.

14 *V. & P.* (L.C.N.S.W.), vol. 1 (1850), p. 151.

15 FitzRoy to Grey, 18 October 1850, C.O. 201/432.

16 Ibid., minute dated 3 April 1851.

17 Ibid., minute dated 5 April 1851.

18 Ibid., minute dated 7 April 1851.

19 Grey to FitzRoy, 26 May 1851, C.O. 201/432.

20 G. W. Rusden to President of M.H.C., 7 November 1851, Victorian Archives, General Branch, Letter Book C.

21 *V. & P.* (L.C.Vic.), (1851-2), p. 545.

22 *Argus*, 31 December 1851. Under Schedule B of 13 & 14 Vic., c. 59, £6,000 annually was reserved for 'Public Worship' in Victoria.

23 *Argus*, 31 December 1851.

24 At the time Jews in the West Indies, Canada and South Australia already had 'full rights' while they remained excluded from the British House of Commons until 1858.

25 *Argus*, 11 September 1852.

26 According to the Census returns there were some 364 Jews in the colony in 1851 and 1,547 in 1854.

27 This apparently would have been the Jews' share of the £6,000 distributed among the Christian denominations on the basis of the 1851 Census returns.

28 Geoffrey Serle, *The Golden Age*, p. 16.

29 *Argus*, 11 September 1852.

30 *V. & P.* (L.C.Vic.), vol. 1 (1852-3), 10 September 1852, p. 181.

31 See Appendix for an analysis of the vote.

32 *Argus*, 1 December 1852.
33 Ibid.
34 J. S. Gregory, 'Church and state in Victoria, 1851-1872' (unpubl. M.A. thesis, University of Melbourne, 1951), pp. 51-2.
35 Ibid.
36 *V. & P.* (L.C.Vic.), vol. 3 (1853-4), p. 612.
37 Ibid.
38 *Argus*, 17 February 1854.
39 Ibid.
40 See Appendix for an analysis of the vote.
41 See *Argus*, 23 February 1854 for a detailed report of the meeting.
42 See also *Jewish Chronicle*, 8 October 1852.
43 *V. & P.* (L.C.Vic.), vol. 3 (1853-4), p. 1089.
44 *Argus*, 18 March 1854.
45 For the Irish support and vote in the House of Commons see *Parl. Deb.* (U.K.), II, vol. 24, p. 793; III, vol. 17, p. 60; vol. 124, p. 621.
46 *Jewish Chronicle*, 9 June 1854; *Argus*, 22 March 1854. Jacob Montefiore arrived in March 1852 from England and, apart from buying gold and acting as a shipping agent, represented the Rothschild interests in the colony. See L. M. Goldman, op. cit., pt 2, p. 426.
47 23 March 1854.
48 Ibid., 24, 27, 28 March 1854.
49 See Serle, op. cit., pp. 14, 132-3, 254, 259; Gregory, op. cit., p. 54.
50 *Jewish Chronicle*, 24 November 1854; Jewish Congregation of Melbourne, Letter Book 1844-56.
51 M.H.C. Minute Book no. 2, entry dated 14 November 1854.
52 Hotham to Gipps, 1 January 1855, C.O. 309/31.
53 The number of Jews in the Census returns were: in 1854, 1,547; in 1857, 2,181; in 1860, 2,903.
54 C.O. 309/31, minute dated 20 March 1855.
55 Russell to Hotham, 21 May 1855, C.O. 309/31.
56 1 June 1854.
57 18 February 1854.
58 See Appendix for analysis of votes on state aid to Jews.
59 *Jewish Chronicle*, 9 June 1854.

9   *Victoria 1856-1859*

1 J. Moore, Assistant Colonial Secretary to M. Cashmore, President of M.H.C., 3 September, 1855, M.H.C. Letter Book, February 1855–November 1859.
2 *Argus*, 14, 15 December 1855.
3 Edward Cohen to W. C. Haines, Chief Secretary, 1 February 1856, M.H.C. Letter Book.
4 M.H.C. Minute Book no. 1, p. 94.
5 For occupational data of Melbourne Jewish Community see 'Register of Births of the Jewish Congregation of Melbourne, Port Phillip' for the 1850s and *Sands & Kenny's Commercial and General Melbourne Directory* (Melbourne, 1858), p. 145.
6 M.H.C. Minute Book no. 1, p. 98.
7 *Argus*, 22 September 1856.
8 Edward Cohen to W. C. Haines, 1 February 1856, M.H.C. Letter Book.
9 J. Moore to Edward Cohen, 12 February 1856, ibid.
10 Thomas McCombie, *The History of the Colony of Victoria: From its settlement to the death of Sir Charles Hotham*, p. 296; J. S. Gregory, 'Church and state in Victoria, 1851-1872', unpubl. M.A. thesis, University of Melbourne, 1951, pp. 71-2.
11 *Parl. Deb.* (L.A.Vic.), vol. 2 (1856-7), p. 706.
12 Gregory, op. cit., pp. 73-4.
13 *Geelong Observer*, 19 August 1856.
14 *Geelong Advertiser*, 22 August 1856.
15 See J. H. Brooke's attack on the 53rd clause in the *Geelong Observer*, 28 June 1856.
16 T. T. à Beckett, *A Defence of State Aid to Religion, passim*, especially p. 5; R. W. Pohlman in *Geelong Advertiser*, 22 August 1856.
17 *Argus*, 1 December 1852.
18 Ibid., 15 December 1856.
19 Ibid., 11 September 1852; *Geelong Observer*, 19 September 1856.
20 Op. cit., p. 18.
21 *Parl. Deb.* (L.A.Vic.), vol. 2 (1856-7), p. 704.
22 Ibid.
23 See *Argus*, 18, 26 June, 8, 12 July, 18, 20, 21 August 1856.

24 Ibid., 16 August 1856.

25 Edward Cohen, *Argus*, 29 August 1856.

26 Ibid., 9 August 1856.

27 Ibid., 18 September 1856.

28 Ibid., 20 September 1856.

29 *Parl. Deb.* (L.A.Vic.), vol. 2 (1857), pp. 693-710.

30 Ibid., p. 697.

31 Ibid., p. 706.

32 Ibid., pp. 707, 971, 1254; Gregory, op. cit., p. 82.

33 *Parl. Deb.* (L.A.Vic.), vol. 2 (1856-7), pp. 982-4.

34 Ibid., p. 982; David Salomons was elected for Greenwich in 1851.

35 Ibid., p. 1066; Gregory, op. cit., p. 85.

36 *Argus*, 15 December 1855.

37 Gregory, op. cit., pp. 82-4.

38 *Parl. Deb.* (L.A.Vic.), vol. 4 (1858-9), p. 819.

39 Ibid.

40 Ibid.; see also *Geelong Observer*, 30 August, 6 September 1856.

41 *Parl. Deb.* (L.A.Vic.), vol. 4 (1858-9), p. 819.

42 Ibid.

43 The £2,000 was distributed among the Jewish congregations of the colony; the Melbourne Hebrew Congregation (Bourke Street), its rival, the East Melbourne Hebrew Congregation (Lonsdale Street), and the Jewish congregations of Ballarat, Geelong, Bendigo and Sandhurst. See M.H.C. Minute Book no. 4, pp. 142-4, 164; Nathan Spielvogel, 'Ballarat Hebrew Congregation', *A.J.H.S.*, vol. 2, p. 352.

44 M.H.C. Minute Book no. 4, pp. 98, 100, 121; M.H.C. Letter Book 1855-9, nos 59/56, 59/57.

45 M.H.C. Letter Book, 1855-9, pp. 254-5.

46 *Jewish Chronicle*, 1 June 1854.

47 See Appendix.

48 *Argus*, 16, 17 February, 18 March 1856.

49 H. G. Turner, *A History of the Colony of Victoria*, vol. 2, pp. 61, 75.

50 *Geelong Observer*, 28 June 1856; *Geelong Advertiser*, 15 August 1856.

10   Conclusion

1 For some examples, see H. M. Sachar, *The Course of Modern Jewish History*, pp. 133-4.

2 L. Loewe (ed.), *The Diaries of Sir Moses and Lady Montefiore*, vol. 1, p. 78.

3 *V. & P.* (L.C.Vic.), vol. 3 (1853-4), p. 1089.

4 S. M. Dubnow, *Die Neueste Geschichte des Juedischen Volkes 1789-1914*, vol. 1, p. 136.

5 Ibid., vol. 2, p. 37.

6 *Parl. Deb.* (U.K.), III, vol. 95, p. 1270. Until the era of Jewish emancipation both Jews and Gentiles would innocently use expressions such as Jewish nation or Jewish people. Only when Jewish emancipation in western and central Europe became associated with, if not predicated on, assimilation to the ruling majority nation, would Jews in the west insist on recognition as a *religion* and describe themselves as of the Israelitic, Hebrew or Mosaic faith, or (in Prussia) as 'Mosaic brethren of the Old Testament faith'; see S. W. Baron, *A Social and Religious History of the Jews*, vol. 2, New York, 1937, p. 262, and S. M. Dubnow, *Neueste Geschichte des Juedischen Volkes*, vol. 2, Berlin, 1920, p. 32. By contrast, the Jews of the 'new world', in the West Indies, the United States of America, Canada, the Australian colonies, who enjoyed equal rights and felt secure, would still speak of themselves occasionally as members of the Jewish or Hebrew nation, perhaps more self-consciously so in the aftermath of the 'Damascus Affair' of 1840.

7 Quoted in I. Porush, 'From Bridge Street to York Street', *A.J.H.S.*, vol. 2, p. 65.

8 Sydney Synagogue Minute Book, 1837-47, p. 31.

9 M. R. Cohen, *Principles of Judaism Arranged in the Form of Question and Answer for the Use of Scholars of Zion House School, Sydney*. (Published by the author and to be obtained from Zion House School

5616-1855.) For the preface, see *A.J.H.S.*, vol. 3, pp. 12-13.

[10] *Commercial Journal*, 5 April 1845.

[11] *Sydney Morning Herald*, 11 November 1858.

[12] Quoted in I. Porush, 'Rev. Herman Hoelzel—the first qualified Jewish Minister in Australia', *A.J.H.S.*, vol. 2, p. 181.

[13] Ibid., p. 192.

[14] *Parl. Deb.* (U.K.), III, vol. 18, pp. 51, 56; vol. 19, p. 1075; vol. 20, p. 235; vol. 58, p. 1049.

[15] Ibid., vol. 98, p. 1293.

[16] Ibid., vol. 57, p. 761; vol. 24, p. 722; vol. 97, p. 1220.

[17] Perhaps T. T. à Beckett in Victoria came close to it.

[18] The Australian colonies were too far away to be reached unassisted by destitute emigrants from the eastern parts of Germany and eastern Europe. Jews in Australia also seem to have done their best to discourage the immigration of 'non-British' Jewish paupers and instructed Jewish emigration societies in England that 'assisted Emigrants should be British born Jews only'. See Edward Cohen to Lewis S. Oppenheim, Secretary of the Jewish Emigration Society, 11 September 1857, M.H.C. Letter Book, February 1855—November 1859.

[19] William Westgarth, *Victoria and the Australian Gold Mines in 1857*, p. 268.

[20] *The History of Tasmania*, vol. 1, p. 214.

[21] Extract from a private letter dated 27 January 1853, *Jewish Chronicle*, 17 June 1853.

[22] Quoted in J. S. Gregory, 'Church and state in Victoria, 1851-1872' (unpubl. M.A. thesis, University of Melbourne, 1951), p. 86.

[23] *Parl. Deb.* (L.A.Vic.), vol. 2 (1856-7), p. 706.

Epilogue

[1] *Eben Saphir* was published in Mainz in 1874; the section relevant to Australia (translated from the Hebrew by I. A. Falk) is in *A.J.H.S.*, vol. 1, pp. 19-22, 43-50, 86-92, 116-20, 153-9, 192-7.

[2] Ibid., p. 45.

[3] U. R. Q. Henriques, 'The Jewish emancipation controversy in nineteenth-century Britain', *Past and Present*, no. 40 (July 1968), pp. 145-6.

Bibliography

1. UNPUBLISHED SOURCES

Mitchell Library, Sydney

Indents of Convict Ships 1790–1824, 1826–35. ('Indents' from 1813 onwards indicate the occupation; from 1826 onwards the religion, of convicts.)

The New South Wales Census taken in the month of November 1828 copied from the original manuscript in the Public Record Office, London, numbered H.O. 10/21 by G. Dwelly in 1932.

Sir Richard Bourke Papers, vol. 2 (letters to Bourke, 1831–45), vol. 6 (letters to his son).

Percy J. Marks Papers (Percy J. Marks Collection of Judaica), Note-books 1–3.

Petition of Members of the Jewish Church in Van Diemen's Land to the Legislative Council of Van Diemen's Land, original MS.

Archives of the Great Synagogue, Sydney

Sydney Synagogue Minute Books, 1837–60.
Sydney Synagogue (Bridge Street) Copy Letters 1840–4.
Sydney Synagogue (York Street) Copy Letters 1844–5.
Sydney Synagogue Letter Book, 1846–59.
Macquarie Street Synagogue Letter Book, 1859–62.
Register of Jewish Births in the Parish of the County of Cumberland (first entry dated 1 November 1826).

Synagogue of the Melbourne Hebrew Congregation, Toorak Road

Minutes of Proceedings of the Jewish Congregational Society, 12 September 1841—8 October 1843.
Minute Book of the Melbourne Hebrew Congregation, no. 1, 1843–53.
Minute Book no. 2, 23 February 1853—10 August 1856.
Minute Book no. 3, 17 August 1855—17 January 1858.
Minute Book no. 4, 14 February 1858—3 May 1863.

Minute Book and Reports of the Sub-Committee of the Melbourne Hebrew Congregation, 1858–71.

Minutes of Committee Meetings of the Melbourne Hebrew Congregation, 24 November 1847—25 September 1852.

Letter Book of the Jewish Congregation of Melbourne, Port Phillip, 5604 A.M. (1844), 1844–56.

Letter Book, February 1855—November 1859.

Register of Births of the Jewish Congregation of Melbourne, Port Phillip, 1844 (first entry is dated 9 July 1841).

Chief Secretary's Archives, Hobart

Van Diemen's Land Duplicate Despatches (inward and outward), 1843, 1844, 1847, 1850, 1851, 1854, 1855.

Minutes of the Legislative Council of Van Diemen's Land, 1837.

Letter Book of the Lieutenant-Governor and Private Secretary, 1851–5.

Hobart Synagogue

Minute Book no. 1 of the Hebrew Congregation in Hobart Town, V.D.L., 16 January 1842—17 August 1851.

Letters of Hobart Hebrew Congregation (mainly correspondence with Sir Moses Montefiore and the London Board of Jewish Deputies in early 1850s).

South Australian Archives

Correspondence of Colonial Secretary with Jacob Levi Montefiore and with Joseph Barrow Montefiore in 1846, 1847, 1851.

Adelaide Synagogue

Minute Book of the Adelaide Hebrew Congregation, 10 September 1848—9 November 1851.

Public Record Office, London—Microfilms

C.O. 323/45: James Stephen's report of 25 January 1828 on the Jamaica Act no. 1940 of 1825 which removed disabilities from the Jews of Jamaica.

C.O. 201/232: Bourke to Stanley, 30 September 1833.

C.O. 209/8(2)/9(1): Russell to Hobson, 9 December 1840.

C.O. 209/20: Shortland to Stanley, 10 May 1843.

C.O. 280/157: Franklin to Stanley, 14 June 1843.

C.O. 201/358: Gipps to Stanley, 13 November 1845.

C.O. 201/369: FitzRoy to Gladstone, 1 October 1846.

C.O. 13/50: Robe to Earl Grey, 15 September 1846.

C.O. 201/432: FitzRoy to Earl Grey, 18 October 1850.

C.O. 201/476: FitzRoy to George Grey, 18 October 1854.

C.O. 309/31: Hotham to George Grey, 1 January 1855; Russell to Hotham, 21 May 1855.

Board of Deputies of British Jews, London
Minute Books nos 1–9, 1760–1864.

Unpublished Theses

Cable, K. J., 'The Church of England in New South Wales and its policy towards education prior to 1880', M.A., University of Sydney, 1952.

Crowley, F. K., 'Aspects of the constitutional conflicts between the two Houses of the Victorian Legislature, 1864–1865', M.A., University of Melbourne, 1947.

Getzler, Israel, 'Neither toleration nor favour: The struggle of the Jewish communities in the Australian colonies for equal religious rights in the 1840s and 1850s', M.A., University of Melbourne, 1960.

Grant, J. A., 'The Victorian election of 1856', B.A. (Hons), University of Melbourne, 1953.

Gregory, J. S., 'Church and state in Victoria, 1851–1872', M.A., University of Melbourne, 1951.

Nadel, G. H., 'Mid-nineteenth century political thought in Australia (New South Wales and Victoria)', M.A., University of Melbourne, 1950.

2. PARLIAMENTARY AND OTHER OFFICIAL PAPERS

Hansard Parliamentary Debates, Second Series, vols 23, 24.

Hansard Parliamentary Debates, Third Series, vols 17–20, 23–4, 33, 39, 56–8, 78, 95–8, 118, 124, 126, 133, 142, 149.

Parliamentary Papers 1850, vol. 36 (despatches and reports related to removal of Jewish disabilities in Jamaica and Canada).

Old Bailey Session Papers, 1783–1810, 1816–20 (Mitchell Library).

Votes and Proceedings of the Legislative Council of New South Wales, 1846, 1853, 1854.

Votes and Proceedings of the Legislative Council of Van Diemen's Land, 1852, 1853.

Votes and Proceedings of the Legislative Council of Victoria, 1851–5.

Victorian Hansard, vols 1–4, 8, 15.

Historical Records of Australia, I, vols 14–15, 18–25.

Statistical Account of Van Diemen's Land or Tasmania, vol. 1, 1804–48. Hobart, 1856.

3. NEWSPAPERS AND PERIODICALS

Argus (Melbourne), 1851–4, 1856
Atlas (Sydney), 1845, 1846
Australian (Sydney), 1830, 1833, 1836, 1844
Australian Jewish Historical Society, *Journal and Proceedings*, vols 1–6
Colonial Times and Tasmanian (Hobart), 1845, 1853-5

Colonist (Sydney), 1836, 1837
Cornwall Chronicle (Launceston), 1843
Cumberland Times and Western Advertiser (Sydney), 1845
Empire (Sydney), 1853, 1854
Examiner (Sydney), 1845
Geelong Advertiser, 1856
Geelong Observer, 1856
Hobart Town Courier, 1845, 1854
Hobart Town Daily Advertiser, 1842, 1843, 1845, 1854
Jewish Chronicle (London), First Series, vol. 1, 12 November 1841—
    15 April 1842
Jewish Chronicle (London), (New Series) 1844–54, vols 1, 2, 18
    October 1844—2 October 1846; vol. 3, 4 June 1847—27 August
    1847
Launceston Examiner, 1843
Melbourne Morning Herald, 1854
Murray's Review (Hobart), 1843
Sentinel (Sydney), 1845
South Australian (Adelaide), 1846–7
South Australian Almanack (Adelaide), 1841, 1846, 1847
South Australian Gazette (Adelaide), 1846
South Australian News (London), 1844
South Australian Register (Adelaide), 1846–8, 1850–1
Sydney Morning Herald, 1844–6, 1849–50, 1853–4, 1856, 1858, 1860
Voice of Jacob (London), vols 1–4, 16 September 1841—26 Septem-
    ber 1845
Voice of Jacob (Sydney), editor George Moss, only three numbers pub-
    lished: 27 May, 24 June, 15 September 1842

4. CONTEMPORARY WORKS

à Beckett, T. T., *A Defence of State Aid to Religion*. Melbourne, 1856.
'A Magistrate' [Colquhoun, Patrick], *A Treatise on the Police of the
    Metropolis*. 4th ed., London, 1797. (First published 1790.)
Arnold, T., *The Christian Duty of Granting the Claims of the Roman
    Catholics*. Oxford, 1829.
———, *Fragment on the Church*. 2nd ed., London, 1845.
Brodzky, M., *Historical Sketch of the Two Melbourne Synagogues*.
    Melbourne, 1877.
Coleridge, S. T., *On the Constitution of the Church and State, Accord-
    ing to the Idea of Each*. 4th ed., London, 1852.
Colquhoun, Patrick, *see* 'A Magistrate'.
Denison, W., *Varieties of Vice-regal Life*. 2 vols. London, 1870.
Duffy, C. G., 'Our first Legislature', *Melbourne Review*, vol. 3 (1878)
    pp. 1–39.
Flanagan, R., *History of New South Wales*. 2 vols. London, 1862.

Gladstone, W. E., *The State in its Relations with the Church*. 3rd ed., London, 1839.

————, *Church Principles considered in their Results*. London, 1840.

Hess, M., *Rome and Jerusalem*, [1860], New York, 1918.

Loewe, L. (ed.), *The Diaries of Sir Moses and Lady Montefiore*. 2 vols. London, 1890.

Macaulay, T. B., *Critical and Historical Essays*. 2 vols. London, 1947.

McCombie, Thomas, *The History of the Colony of Victoria: From its settlement to the death of Sir Charles Hotham*. London, 1858.

Mansfield, Ralph, *Analytical View of the Census of New South Wales for the Year 1841*. Sydney, 1841.

————, *Analytical View of the Census of New South Wales for the Year 1846*. Sydney, 1847.

Merivale, H., *Lectures on Colonization and Colonies, Delivered before the University of Oxford in 1839, 1840 and 1841*. London, 1861.

Report of the Committee of the Sydney Synagogue 1845, Australian Jewish Historical Society, Sydney, 1944.

Stanley, A. P., *Life and Correspondence of Thomas Arnold*. London, 1852.

Trower, C. F., *An Answer to the Speech of Sir Robert Peel in the House of Commons on Friday February 11 1848 upon the Second Reading of the Jewish Disabilities Bill*. London, 1848.

West, J., *The History of Tasmania*. 2 vols. Launceston, 1852.

Westgarth, W., *Victoria, Late Australia Felix*. Edinburgh, 1853.

————, *Victoria and the Australian Gold Mines in 1857*. London, 1857.

5. LATER WORKS

Australian Dictionary of Biography, see Pike, D. (ed.).

Baron, S. W., *A Social and Religious History of the Jews*. 3 vols. New York, 1937.

————, *The Jewish Community*. 3 vols. Philadelphia, 1942.

————, 'The Modern Age' in Leo W. Schwarz (ed.), *Great Ages and Ideas of the Jewish People*. New York, 1957.

————, 'The Jewish question in the nineteenth century', *Journal of Modern History*, vol. 10 (1938), pp. 51–65.

————, *Die Judenfrage auf dem Wiener Kongress. Auf Grund von zum Teil ungedruckten Quellen dargestellt*. Vienna and Berlin, 1920.

Blacket, B. J., *History of South Australia*. Adelaide, 1911.

Blau, J. L. and Baron, S. W. (eds), *The Jews in the United States 1790–1840, A Documentary History*, vol. 1. New York and London, 1963.

Clark, C. M. H., *Select Documents in Australian History, 1788–1850*. Sydney, 1950.

————, *Select Documents in Australian History, 1851–1900*. Sydney, 1955.

————, 'The origins of the convicts transported to eastern Australia, 1787–1852', *Historical Studies, Australia and New Zealand,* no. 26 (1956), pp. 121–35, 314–27.

Collins, I., *Liberalism in the Nineteenth Century.* London, 1957.

Crawford, R. M., *Australia.* London, 1952.

Dubnow, S. M., *Die Neueste Geschichte des Juedischen Volkes 1789–1914.* 2 vols. Berlin, 1920.

————, *Nationalism and History.* Philadelphia, 1958.

Eggleston, F. W., *Reflections of an Australian Liberal.* Melbourne, 1953.

Engelman, U. Z., *The Rise of the Jew in the Modern World.* New York, 1944.

Evatt, H. V., *Liberalism in Australia.* Sydney, 1918.

Fabian, A., 'Early days of South Australian Jewry', *A.J.H.S.,* vol. 2, pp. 127–44.

Fenton, J., *History of Tasmania.* London, 1894.

Finkelstein, L. (ed.), *The Jews: Their history, culture and religion.* 2 vols. New York, 1949.

Fitzpatrick, B., *British Imperialism and Australia.* London, 1939.

Fitzpatrick, K., *Sir John Franklin in Tasmania 1837–1843.* Melbourne, 1949.

Freedman, H. and Super, A. N., *One Hundred Years: The story of the Melbourne Hebrew Congregation, 1841–1941.* Melbourne, 1941.

Freedman, M. (ed.), *A Minority in Britain: Social studies of the Anglo-Jewish community.* London, 1955.

Glass, S. B., 'The Jews' Relief (English) Act 1858 and Australian re-action to same', *A.J.H.S.,* vol. 1, pp. 8–18.

Grant, J. and Serle, G., *The Melbourne Scene 1803–1956.* Melbourne, 1957.

Greenwood, G. (ed.), *Australia: A social and political history.* Sydney, 1955.

Halévy, E., *A History of the English People in the Nineteenth Century,* vols 3, 4. London, 1951.

Hancock, W. K., *Australia.* London, 1930.

Henriques, H. S. Q., *The Jews and the English Law.* London, 1908.

Henriques, Ursula, *Religious Toleration in England 1787–1833.* London, 1961.

————, 'The Jewish emancipation controversy in nineteenth-century Britain', *Past and Present,* no. 40 (July 1968), pp. 126–46.

Hertz, J. H., *The First Pastoral Tour to the Jewish Communities of the British Overseas Dominions.* Oxford, 1924.

Hodder, E., *History of South Australia.* 2 vols. London, 1893.

Hyamson, A. M., *A History of the Jews in England.* 2nd ed., London, 1928.

Katz, J., *Tradition and Crisis: Jewish society at the end of the middle ages.* 2nd ed., Jerusalem, 1963.

Knaplund, P., *James Stephen and the Colonial Office 1813–1847.* Madison, 1953.

Krohn, Helga, *Die Juden in Hamburg 1800–1850.* Frankfurt am Main, 1967.

Linz, C. C., *The Establishment of a National System of Education in New South Wales.* Melbourne, 1938.

Lipman, V. D., *Social History of the Jews in England 1850–1950.* London, 1954.

Mahler, R., *Jewish Emancipation: A selection of documents.* New York, 1941.

Main, J. M., 'Making Constitutions in New South Wales and Victoria, 1853–1854', *Historical Studies, Australia and New Zealand,* no. 27 (1957), pp. 369–86.

Marks, P. J., 'Early Jewish education in Sydney, New South Wales', *A.J.H.S.,* vol. 1, pp. 25–42.

Medding, P. Y., *From Assimilation to Group Survival: A political and sociological study of an Australian Jewish community.* Melbourne, 1968.

Melbourne, A. C. V., *William Charles Wentworth.* London, 1934.

———, *Early Constitutional Development in Australia: New South Wales 1788–1856.* London, 1934.

Morley, J., *The Life of William Ewart Gladstone.* vol. 1. London, 1922.

Munz, H., *Jews in South Australia 1836–1936: An historical outline.* Adelaide, 1936.

O'Brien, E. M., *The Foundation of Australia 1786–1800: A study in English practice and penal colonization in the eighteenth century.* 2nd ed., Sydney 1950.

Oeser, O. A. and Hammond, S. B. (eds), *Social Structure and Personality in a City.* London, 1954.

Picciotto, J., *Sketches of Anglo-Jewish History.* London, 1875.

Pike, D., *Paradise of Dissent: South Australia 1829–1857.* London, 1957; 2nd ed., Melbourne, 1967.

———, (ed.), *Australian Dictionary of Biography.* Vols 1–3. Melbourne, 1966–9.

Porush, I., 'The story of state aid to Jewish establishments in New South Wales', *A.J.H.S.,* vol. 1, pp. 337–55; vol. 2, pp. 29–38.

Price, C. A., *Jewish Settlers in Australia.* Canberra, 1964.

Roth, C., *A History of the Jews in England.* 2nd ed., Oxford, 1949.

Ruggiero, G. de, *The History of European Liberalism.* London, 1927.

Ruppin, A., *The Jews in the Modern World.* London, 1934.

Rusden, G. W., *History of Australia.* 3 vols. London, 1883.

Sachar, H. M., *The Course of Modern Jewish History.* London, 1958.

Schapiro, S. J., *Liberalism and the Challenge of Fascism.* New York, 1949.

Schappes, M. U., *Documentary History of Jews in the United States 1654–1875.* New York, 1952.

Serle, G., *The Golden Age: A history of the colony of Victoria 1851–1861*. Melbourne, 1963.

Shaw, A. G. L., *The Story of Australia*. London, 1955.

Sweetman, E., *Constitutional Development of Victoria 1851–6*. Melbourne, 1921.

Townsley, W. A., *The Struggle for Self-government in Tasmania 1842–1856*. Hobart, 1951.

Turner, H. G., *A History of the Colony of Victoria*. 2 vols. London, 1904.

Ward, R., *The Australian Legend*. Melbourne, 1958.

Wolff, H. I., 'Governor Bourke and the Sydney (Bridge Street) Synagogue', *A.J.H.S.*, vol. 1, pp. 143–5.

Index